THESE SEVEN SICKNESSES

The Sophocles Plays:
OEDIPUS, IN TRACHIS,
IN COLONUS,
PHILOKTETES, AJAX,
ELEKTRA, ANTIGONE

Adapted by
Sean Graney

D1568992

BROADWAY PLAY PUBLISHING INC
224 E 62nd St, NY NY 10065-8201
212 772-8334 fax: 212 772-8358
BroadwayPlayPubl.com

THESE SEVEN SICKNESSES
© Copyright 2013 by Sean Graney

All rights reserved. This work is fully protected under the copyright laws of the United States of America. No part of this publication may be photocopied, reproduced, stored in a retrieval system, or transmitted, in any form or by any means, electronic, mechanical, recording, or otherwise, without the prior permission of the publisher. Additional copies of this play are available from the publisher.

Written permission is required for live performance of any sort. This includes readings, cuttings, scenes, and excerpts. For amateur and stock performances, please contact Broadway Play Publishing Inc. For all other rights contact Mark Orsini, Bret Adams Ltd, 448 W 44th St, NY NY 10036, 212 765-5630, morsini@bretadamsltd.net.

First printing: April 2013
Second printing: March 2015
I S B N: 978-0-88145-565-6

Book design: Marie Donovan
Page make-up: Adobe Indesign
Typeface: Palatino
Printed and bound in the U S A

ABOUT THE AUTHOR

Sean Graney is a playwright, adapter and director based in Chicago, IL. He is the Founding Director of The Hypocrites, a company where he served as Artistic Director for 14 years. He has won several Joseph Jefferson Awards for Directing and Adaptation, and was a participant in the N E A/T C G Career Development Program for Directors in 2004.

THESE SEVEN SICKNESSES was first produced as SOPOCLES: SEVEN SICKNESSES by The Hypocrites (Halena Kays*, Artistic Director; Megan Wildebour*, Managing Director; Sean Graney*, Founding Artistic Director) at the Chopin Theatre, Chicago, IL, opening on 11 September 2011. The cast and creative contributors were:

Erin Barlow
Ryan Bourque
Walter Briggs
Geoff Button*
Tien Doman
Lindsey Gavel
Sarah Jackson
Maximillian Lapine
Shannon Matesky
Robert McLean*
Zeke Sulkes
Jeff Trainor

Stage manager...................................... Miranda Anderson*
Technical director................................ Michael Smallwood
Music director.. Kevin O'Donnell*
Scenic design....................... Tom Burch & Maria DeFabo*
Costume design...Alison Siple*
Lighting design .... Jared Moore*
Sound design..Stephen Ptacek
Properties design..Maria DeFabo*
Violence design .... Ryan Bourque
Mask design ....Kristina Herne

Make up/gore design ....Mary Williamson
& Christine Conley

* denotes company member

THESE SEVEN SICKNESSES was first produced in New York at The Flea Theater (Jim Simpson, Artistic Director; Carol Ostrow, Producing Director). The cast and creative contributors were:

Tiffany Abercrombie
Matt Barbot
Yoni Ben-Yehuda
Satomi Blair
Dave Brown
Allison Buck
Charlotte Bydwell
Holly Chou
Jenelle Chu
Ugo Chukwu
Alexander Cook
Tommy Crawford
Eloïse Eonnet
Bobby Foley
Katherine Folk-Sullivan
Glenna Grant
Cleo Gray
Alex Grubbs
Grant Harrison
Victoria Haynes
Cameran Hebb
Alex Herrald
Miles Jacoby
Betsy Lippitt
Sean McIntyre
Kate Michaud

Seth Moore
Eric Olson
Victor Joel Ortiz
Jeff Ronan
Marie Claire Roussel
Olivia Stoker
Stephen Stout
Liz Tancredi
Will Turner
Tony Vo
Nate Washburn
Akyiaa Wilson

Director	Ed Sylvanus Iskander
Dramaturg	Greg VanHorn
Set design	Julia Noulin-Merat
Lighting design	Carl Wiemann
Costume design	Loren Shaw
Sound design	Patrick Metzger
Fight director	Michael Wieser
Music director	David Dabbon
Production voice/speech coach	Amy Jo Jackson
Makeup design	Tiffany Abercrombie
Assistant set design	John Jalandoni
Assistant to set design	Jennifer Woo
Assistant costume design	Maeve Kelly
Photography	Laura Kirsch
Stage manager	Edward Herman
Stage manager	Kara Kaufman
Set design intern	Laura Hoffman
Resident director	Tom Costello
Resident director	Ben Kamine

CHARACTERS & SETTING

OEDIPUS
ANTIGONE
CREON
ISMENE
THE BLIND SEER
JOCASTA
POLYNEICES
THESEUS
HAEMON
SICK MAN
ETEOKLES
PHILOKTETES
ELEKTRA
DEJANIRA
HYLLUS
IOLE
AJAX
ODYSSEUS
ORESTES
NEOPTOLEMUS
HERAKLES
CHRYSOTHEMIS
CLYTEMNESTRA
AGAMEMNON
TEKMESSA
EURYSAKES
AEGISTHUS

MENELAUS
NURSE, *could be divided among a group of people*
NEW NURSE
THE CARRIER
A FLOCK OF SHEEP

You may double roles, for smaller cast size, or not.

Sort of like a hospital, or a morgue. Sort of like a catastrophe. Enjoy!

Halves:

Of Theban Rule: OEDIPUS, IN COLONUS, ANTIGONE

The Golden Bow: IN TRACHIS, PHILOKTETES, AJAX, ELEKTRA

PROLOGUE

(At lease one NURSE, *but may be as many as needed, enters the space and turn on the lights. Medical equipment litters this place.)*

NURSE: Another day.

(NEW NURSE enters.)

NEW NURSE: Hello.

NURSE: Are you the new one?

NEW NURSE: Yes, I think so.

NURSE: There's one thing to know.
This sickness.
There's no cure.

NEW NURSE: Well, what do we do?

NURSE: Just work.
Don't get involved and work.

(Leads immediately into...)

.

PART 1: HONOR LOST
ACT 1: OEDIPUS

(SICK MAN *enters, coughing violently and collapses. The* NURSES *rush to her.* OEDIPUS *and* ANTIGONE *enter,* ANTIGONE *carries flowers.)*

NURSE: King Oedipus.

OEDIPUS: Hello.

ANTIGONE: How bad is he?

NURSE: He won't make it.

OEDIPUS: Antigone, go home please.
Antigone, now, please.

ANTIGONE: Yes father. *(She exits.)*

OEDIPUS: What can I do?

NEW NURSE: Nothing.
I think.

OEDIPUS: Nothing?
There must be something.

(SICK MAN *starts to cough and convulse.)*

OEDIPUS: Hold on, man, hold on.
I will help you.
I solved the Riddle of the Hellbitch,
And I can lift this sickness from the city,
Hold my hand.
Your pain is my pain.

(The SICK MAN *stops convulsing.)*

OEDIPUS: Did she die?

NEW NURSE: No, she sleeps.

*(*NURSE *gives* SICK MAN *a shot.)*

OEDIPUS: A blight upon our crops.
A blight upon our flocks.
A blight upon our pregnant wives,
Who give birth to nothing but bloody amalgamations
   of putrid carnage.
They crowd the streets.
Laying in decay.
Pray before polluted altars.
Pushing their still-living children upon fires,
That burn through their houses.
No one will make it, will they?

NEW NURSE: It's hard to say.

OEDIPUS: They all want me to end this plague.

NURSE: You are their King.

OEDIPUS: But what can I do?

(Enter CREON.*)*

CREON: Oedipus.

OEDIPUS: Creon, Brother-in-law,
What things have you discovered about this sickness?

CREON: Good things Oedipus.

OEDIPUS: You saw the Oracle?

CREON: Oh yeah.

OEDIPUS: What did the Oracle say?

CREON: We shouldn't discuss this here.
Let's go to some place private.

OEDIPUS: My ears are those of my children.
What can be said to me can be said to all.

CREON: Don't be so proud Oedipus.

OEDIPUS: You don't be so proud.

CREON: Okay.

OEDIPUS: What did the Oracle say?

CREON: The Oracle said, "We need to strike out this
  pollution that infects our blood
For we safely harbor the pathogen that feeds on our
  lives."

OEDIPUS: What does that mean?

CREON: The Oracle said banishment,
Take blood for blood taken,
For this infected blood bloodies our bloody people.

OEDIPUS: What does that mean?

CREON:
It means that a person is responsible for this scourge.
And we house him.

OEDIPUS: Here?

CREON: Yes.

OEDIPUS: Here?

CREON: Yes here.

OEDIPUS: Who is the person causing the scourge?

CREON: The Oracle said it is the same man who killed
  our strong former King Laius.

OEDIPUS: But Laius was killed by a group of
  highwaymen, not one man.

CREON: That is what we were told,
But the Oracle disagrees.

OEDIPUS: That was so long ago,
We could never find his murderer now.

CREON: I was told,
The one who seeks, shall find.
The one who hides is blind.

OEDIPUS: What does that mean?

CREON: We should look for the murderer,
And we will find him.

OEDIPUS: What do you know about Laius' murder?

CREON:
He was abroad, going to Delphi but never returned.

OEDIPUS:
Who reported it was a group of highwaymen?

CREON: One of Laius' servants escaped the melee.

(SICK MAN *quietly coughs and* NURSES *tend to him.*)

OEDIPUS: Was this investigated?

CREON: Yes briefly,
But the Hellbitch then held us under her tyranny,
And we needed to deal with the hardships she
    wrought.

OEDIPUS: I solved the riddle of the Hellbitch.

CREON: And that was awesome.

OEDIPUS: What should we do, Creon?

CREON: I think we should call the Blind Seer.

OEDIPUS: The Blind Seer?
Will she come?
I was told she renounced us
And promised never to return.

CREON: I think I can convince her.

OEDIPUS: Thank you, Creon.
I love you like my brother.

CREON: And I you.
My sister and our city are in good hands.
I know you will cure us of this wretched disease.

OEDIPUS: I will find this man,
And we will push this illness from our city.
If not, I am fit to rule over a desert wasteland,
Not a place where proud people stand.

(OEDIPUS *tends to* SICK MAN. CREON *calls some one about*
THE BLIND SEER, *the* NURSES *sing while they clean, using a
bottle of bleach.*)

[The Song Of Knowledge Unknown]

CREON: Blind Seer will be arriving right about...now.

(THE BLIND SEER *is pushed onto stage in a wheelchair as*
CREON *exits.*)

THE BLIND SEER: Whoa whoa whoa!

OEDIPUS: Blind Seer, who sees all,
Knower of the obscured riddles,
I ask you, what plagues our city.

THE BLIND SEER: What plagues what city?
Where am I?

OEDIPUS: Thebes.

THE BLIND SEER: Oh Thebes.
Then if you could just point me to the door.

OEDIPUS: Wait Blind Seer.

THE BLIND SEER: Thebes is not where I should be.

OEDIPUS: Please help us.

THE BLIND SEER: And you are King Oedipus?

OEDIPUS: I am.
It is said that we need to find the murderer of our
strong former King Laius,
To save ourselves from this defilement.

I have devoted all my power to finding this murderer
and purging him from our city,
To end this sickness...

THE BLIND SEER: *(Interrupting)*
Blah blah blah.
Oh to wish to be wise,
When you know not what you want to know.
I have long since forgotten this city.
So let this city forget me.

OEDIPUS: Why won't you help us?

THE BLIND SEER: Let me go home.
Show me to the door.
I shall bear my suffering.
And you shall bear yours.

OEDIPUS: Tell us what you know.
I warn you, if you withhold any knowledge that can
    help us...

THE BLIND SEER: What, or what?
What will you do to an old blind woman?

OEDIPUS: Please speak,
Let us know what you know.
(He kneels.)
We all kneel before your greatness.
I, a King, kneel before you.
I know you can't see, but this is quite a humbling sight.

THE BLIND SEER:
If I spoke, you would soon ask me to not speak.
So please listen to your future self and heed his
    warning.

OEDIPUS: Please have some compassion.

THE BLIND SEER: I have compassion
But you would be better served to lose your
    compassion.

Let your subjects rot,
That is what great Kings do.

OEDIPUS:
Great Kings would never display such cruelty.

THE BLIND SEER: None of them display it,
But all the great ones feel it.

(OEDIPUS *gets out a medical instrument, like a defibrillator.*)

OEDIPUS: If you want to see cruelty,
That I will gladly show to you alone.
I hold in my hand an instrument,
And I am willing to use this instrument.

THE BLIND SEER:
No one can make the truth fall from another's mouth.

OEDIPUS: We will see if that is true.
Tell me what you know.

(OEDIPUS *tortures* THE BLIND SEER.)

NEW NURSE: Hey.

NURSE: Don't get involved.

(*The* NURSES *go about their business.*)

THE BLIND SEER: I will speak if you will listen.

OEDIPUS: I will listen.

THE BLIND SEER: Look about, what do you see?

OEDIPUS: Look about, here?

THE BLIND SEER:
Yes, gaze around and report what you see.

OEDIPUS: I see myself, my children, my dying city.

THE BLIND SEER: You may be blinder than I.
Do you see your line?

OEDIPUS: My line?

(THE BLIND SEER slowly stands from her wheel chair, it gets creepy.)

THE BLIND SEER:
Do you see you are a foe to your friend,
A double foe fiend to thy unknown kin,
The living and the dead.

OEDIPUS: Are you being confusing on purpose?

THE BLIND SEER: Do you see you are chained to the
    curse of your mother and father,
Do you see that you and your children are of one line,
One point on one line.

OEDIPUS: I don't.

THE BLIND SEER: And do you see where you will go,
How this city will long since drive you out?

OEDIPUS: This city will not drive me out.

THE BLIND SEER:
And do you see that you will lose all that you see,
And wander into endless night.
And see this greatly King fiend,
The man you seek is here.
He seems a stranger,
But you will see, he is a native.
Then you will soon see him a foreigner again,
Using a staff for eyes.
And his children, his inmates,
He shall find them as close as sisters.
And the woman who calls him husband,
Shall return him to her breast,
Like he was long before their wedding day.
And his father's blood,
Not only rages in his veins,
But also stains his hands.
So you see Oedipus the great,
Now Oedipus the ragdoll with his eyes unsewn.

(OEDIPUS *throws* THE BLIND SEER *back into her wheelchair.*)

OEDIPUS: Tell me who is the killer of the strong former
   King Laius.

THE BLIND SEER: Alright.
What doesn't lie?

OEDIPUS: An honest man.

THE BLIND SEER: What else?
What object fool?
What object doesn't lie?

OEDIPUS: A mirror.

THE BLIND SEER: Get a mirror and I will show you the
cause of the scourge.

(OEDIPUS *looks in a mirror.*)

THE BLIND SEER: What do you see?

OEDIPUS: I see me.
A compassionate ruler man.

THE BLIND SEER:
No, you see a liar and you see the question.
And you see the answer of the scourge.

OEDIPUS: I see now.
Clear as rain.

THE BLIND SEER: You do?

OEDIPUS: I see that Creon called.

THE BLIND SEER: Yes.

OEDIPUS: And I see you and he are co-conspiritors,
Out to transplant me from my rightly won throne,
For answering the Riddle of the Hellbitch.
I see Creon's evil tricks.
He plays the records and you dance the dance.

THE BLIND SEER: Then you are more blind than I.

OEDIPUS: Leave me auspex of un-terminated night,
You are no master of me or anyone who sees the sun.
Leave me.

THE BLIND SEER: I humbly thank you,
And happy birthday sir.

OEDIPUS: It is not my birthday.

THE BLIND SEER: Yes, it is, and the start of your death.
Know me, the Blind Seer.
And later, in a day or so,
Tell me then, what you see.
And tell me then, who is the blind one.
This is the door no?
(She exits.)

(Enter CREON.)

CREON: How did that go?

OEDIPUS: Creon, do you have such a strong need to
take my crown that you make a fool of me?
To rot my image in front of my children.
To send a serpent to poison my sleep.

CREON: What?

OEDIPUS: I see your blinding hate.

CREON: What?

OEDIPUS: Did you call the Blind Seer?

CREON: Yes, I did.

OEDIPUS: Did you tell me to consult the Blind Seer?

CREON: And what did she say?

OEDIPUS:
That the murderer of our strong former King Laius,
Stands before you.

CREON: Where?

OEDIPUS: Here.

CREON: *(Pointing to audience member)*
That lady?

OEDIPUS: No.

CREON: Me?

OEDIPUS: No, me.

CREON: Really.

OEDIPUS: Yes.

CREON:
And so, you think I conspired with the Blind Seer?

OEDIPUS: Yes, to plant doubt in the people,
To get them to reject me as their King,
Then you could take my throne.

CREON: The throne is my sister's,
And she gives it to you.

OEDIPUS: Yes,
She does,
But I rule justly.

CREON:
True, so why would I want to disrupt your just rule,
When you give me all I desire,
And welcome me as a brother?

OEDIPUS: I don't know yet.

CREON: There must be some misunderstanding.
Why would The Blind Seer accuse you?
The Blind Seer speaks in circle riddles.
It gets very confusing.

OEDIPUS:
Defend yourself, rather than slandering the Blind Seer.

CREON: I am not slandering the Blind Seer,
For she always speaks the truth.
I am saying that she sometimes obscures the truth in

double talk,
So it reveals itself when we are ready to hear it.

OEDIPUS: Keep talking.

CREON: Look, if I wanted to rule
Why would I waste so much time trying to convince
    you that you were the murderer.
Why wouldn't I go directly to Jocasta?

OEDIPUS: I don't know, yet.

CREON: Truth is Oedipus,
When Jocasta and I were younger,
I had a chance to govern the throne,
When the life left our father.
But I bestowed the throne to Jocasta,
Who was eager to rule.
Trust me,
I just don't want to be king.
I get all the benefits of royalty without the weight.

NURSE: The logic seems sound, Oedipus.

OEDIPUS: Hmmm.

CREON: I know things are confusing.

OEDIPUS: They are.
This is distracting me from concentrating on finding
    Laius' murderer
And ending the scourge.

CREON: What do you need?

OEDIPUS:
Look, I don't know what is true and what is a lie.

CREON: Okay.

OEDIPUS: I'll need to ask you to leave,
Until this can be sorted through.

CREON: Leave, like here?

OEDIPUS: Yes, just for a little bit.

CREON: Like give you time to think?

OEDIPUS: Yeah, but not just here,
I mean like leave Thebes.

CREON: Are you like banishing me?

OEDIPUS: Just for a while,
Until I can sort through all this.

CREON: You can't do that Oedipus.

OEDIPUS: Yes I can.

CREON: No, not really.

OEDIPUS: I am your King?

CREON: The King of these people,
But you are my sister's husband,
And there your rule over me ends.

OEDIPUS: Do you hear him?

NURSE: Yes.

CREON: Am I not a person,
Don't I deserve your compassion.
Would you throw me into the desert wasteland and
    leave me for dead?

OEDIPUS: Be ruled by me.
You must be banished.

Or you shall face a treasonous death.

CREON: No.

OEDIPUS: You must, it's an order.

CREON: I won't.

OEDIPUS: Either leave, or I will force you out.

CREON: No.

(CREON and OEDIPUS fight. Enter JOCASTA.)

JOCASTA: Gentlemen, please, have you no shame.
The whole land lies in sickly ruin,

And you two fight like it's a playground.
What is wrong with you two?

CREON: Jocasta, sister, he wants to banish me.

OEDIPUS: Jocasta, wife, I have caught your brother in
the black magic art of treason.

CREON: May I find slow and cruel death if that is true.

JOCASTA: Oedipus, this is outrageous.

OEDIPUS: I don't know if it's outrageous until I can
gather the meaning of some strange events.

JOCASTA: Oedipus, please, don't banish him.
Please show some grace.
Please.

OEDIPUS: Fine.
Go.
You matter no more to me, Creon.
Be it death, or banishment or boredom you are
subjected to,
Know you have gained my hatred.

CREON: Such tempers fit not to rule my lord.

OEDIPUS: You starting again?

(*Exit* CREON.)

JOCASTA: Oedipus, what happened?

OEDIPUS: Strange council killed my hope and perverted
my passion Jocasta.

JOCASTA: The details, love.

OEDIPUS: Creon wants my throne.

JOCASTA: No, Oedipus, you are mistaken.
Creon does not want the throne.
He and I have had this conversation throughout our
lives.
He doesn't want the burden of ruling others.

OEDIPUS: Creon called the Blind Seer,
And the Blind Seer reported,
Through riddles,
That I was the murderer of your dead former husband.

JOCASTA: And you think that makes a conspiracy,

Between Creon and the Blind Seer?

OEDIPUS: Yes.

JOCASTA: My husband, although many believe
All words that fly from the mouth of the Blind Seer are
    gilded in truth,
I know for certain,
The Blind Seer is not always right.

OEDIPUS: How do you know this?

JOCASTA: A long long time ago
She gave us an omen
My strong former husband Laius and I
The Blind Seer portended that Laius was to be slain by
    his own son,
A son of mine.
And she reported vile actions this child would perform
    with me.
We did have a child.
But when it was three days old,
Laius ripped it from my arms,
Pierced its ankles,
And had another bring it far from here, and hang him
    from a tree.
I thought it barbaric,
But I could do nothing to stop him.
And as we know Laius was murdered by highwaymen,
    robbers, foreigners;
At a place where three roads meet.
Not natives, not his son.
So my husband,

As you can see the prophet prophesizes foolish
  prophesies.

OEDIPUS: What did you say?

JOCASTA: When?

OEDIPUS: My brain burns!

JOCASTA: What?

OEDIPUS: Ahhhhh!

JOCASTA: What is it?

OEDIPUS: Oh Jocasta my head burns.
My brain is on fire.
I can't see from the fire in my eyes.
Get me water.

(NURSES *gives* OEDIPUS *water, trying to calm him down.*)

OEDIPUS: A place where three roads meet?

JOCASTA: What?

OEDIPUS: Laius was murdered at a place where three
  roads meet?

JOCASTA: Yes.
Tell me what is happening

OEDIPUS: I'm afraid my love,
I'm afire my love.

JOCASTA: Calm down my King.

OEDIPUS: What did Laius look like?

JOCASTA: Strong.
White hair.
Your build.

OEDIPUS: Did he have a beard?

JOCASTA: No

OEDIPUS: Was he slain alone?

JOCASTA: No. There were five that were slain

OEDIPUS: Five?

JOCASTA: What Oedipus what?

OEDIPUS: Highwaymen killed Laius?

JOCASTA: Yes.

OEDIPUS: Who reported this?

JOCASTA: A slave reported that she saw the whole thing
from the bushes.

(SICK MAN *coughs during this dialogue, but is ignored.*)

OEDIPUS: A slave?
Do we keep him?

JOCASTA:
He returned at the moment you entered the city,
And he begged to be released.

OEDIPUS: More water.
My eyes burn.
Where is the slave?

JOCASTA: He went to the mountains

OEDIPUS: Can we send for him? Can we please?
Is that all right?

JOCASTA: Of course my love.

OEDIPUS: I think the Blind Seer can see!

(The NURSES *give* OEDIPUS *a physical and calm him down.*)

NEW NURSE: Relax.

NURSE: Talk us through this.

OEDIPUS: My father was King of Corinth,
And my mother…

NURSE: Was queen.

OEDIPUS: Yeah. Yeah.
And there in Corinth I was held in high regard.

NEW NURSE: Of course.

OEDIPUS: Then one night.
There was a banquet,
And one of the men filled with a little too much of the
    grain liquor,
And was bothering a woman of reasonable
    attractiveness,
But of firm puritan morals.
So I stopped him, embarrassed he was more than
    anything.
Probably a little ashamed,
For this young lady was young, and he wasn't in the
    prime of his life.
So he said to me, "You bastard slave of the woods.
Your father is your owner,
He owns you like his sheep."
It was drunken shouting, embarrassed banter,
But still something rang in my stomach.
I asked my parents,
They tried to comfort me.

NEW NURSE: Saying that their love could come from
    none but parents.

OEDIPUS: But it stank, like venom in my bloodstream.
So I went privately to seek advice of the Oracles
I thought they might help me, out of pity.

NURSE: Did they?

OEDIPUS: No. But perhaps.
My questions weren't answered,
But I got answers to questions unasked.
Grievous answers to grievous questions I didn't even
    know existed.
You know, woes, laments, mourning grief,
Agony over agony over agony.

NURSE: Go on.

OEDIPUS: The Oracle said
"I will dirty my mother's bed with my loathsome seed

And kill the man who fathered me"
So I ran, I never went home, afraid of the prophecy,
Knowing I was going to kill my father and bed my
    mother.
A thought too great to bear.
I ran and ran.
But it's funny, right, outrun the Oracles?
I didn't know where I was running.
I came upon a crossroads,
Where three roads crossed, sure enough.
And I stayed not knowing where to go,
In the middle of the road.
Panting, panicked...

NEW NURSE: Go on

OEDIPUS: A cart came up.
Five men total.
The herald told me to move,
And hit me with his staff.
Can you believe that?
A man obviously afraid of something, to abuse me so.

NEW NURSE: Not very kind

OEDIPUS: No
So...
Without thinking...
I grabbed the man's staff,
And struck him so hard his head parted like a pod
bursting a pink flower.
Then the old man in front of the cart stood.
With threat.
And I acted so quickly and struck him.
Not thinking at all,
Exhausted from running,
Scared of my fate.
The old man's head bled its golden blood,

Three others charged at me,
I fought them off.

NURSE: What happened next?

OEDIPUS: Then they all lay slain.

NURSES: Oh Oedipus.

OEDIPUS: I know.
I am lost.
I pollute the bed of him I slew.
I am the plague.

JOCASTA: No no no.
The slave we sent for,
The slave will arrive shortly,
The slave will alleviate your fear,
The slave will validate the opposite of what you
   suspect.
These torments are for naught.
You will see.

OEDIPUS: Will I see?

JOCASTA: You will see.
Come inside.
Come inside my love.
I will comfort thee.

OEDIPUS: I shall find no comfort in calamity

(*Exit* OEDIPUS. *Enter* THE CARRIER.)

THE CARRIER: Hello.

NEW NURSE: Hey.

THE CARRIER:
Could you tell me, is this the land of Oedipus.

NURSE: It is.

NEW NURSE:
And this is the mother of his sons and daughters.

JOCASTA: What can I do for you?

THE CARRIER: May my arrival bring blessing.

JOCASTA: It may.

THE CARRIER: Don't worry,
I bring not want or need,
But news.
I am a Carrier.

JOCASTA: Where from?

THE CARRIER:
The land where your husband was raised.
The land in which he is now King.

JOCASTA: No.

Polybus, Oedipus' father, rules there.

THE CARRIER: As time would have it,
The only space Polybus rules is his grave ma'am.

JOCASTA: Oedipus' Father is dead?

THE CARRIER: Yes ma'am.

JOCASTA: Why this is happy news.

THE CARRIER: Alright ma'am
Polybus was a just and jovial leader,
We must mourn for him.
We would like Oedipus to return to lead the rites,
And take the throne.

JOCASTA: Oedipus

(*Enter* OEDIPUS.)

OEDIPUS: What Jocasta?

JOCASTA: Listen to this Carrier.

THE CARRIER: My great Oedipus,
I bear two-fold contradictory news,
Your father has died, sir.

OEDIPUS: My father is dead?

THE CARRIER: Yes sir.

OEDIPUS: How did his life come to pass?

THE CARRIER: Old age sir.

OEDIPUS: Did any malady strike him?

THE CARRIER: Just life, sir.
Not even grief.
Just the course of life ended.
No foul play,
Other than that of time.

OEDIPUS: I didn't kill my father?

THE CARRIER:
No sir, unless you can take credit for nature's work.

OEDIPUS: I cannot.

JOCASTA: Seers see mistakes, see.

OEDIPUS: I did not kill my father.

JOCASTA: We are our own masters my lord.
Prophecies are fear tactics of scared old men.

OEDIPUS: No longer shall I be ruled by fear.
I did not kill my father or bed my mother.

(JOCASTA and OEDIPUS kiss for a long time.)

OEDIPUS: But my mother still lives Carrier?

THE CARRIER: Yes sir she does.

JOCASTA: But are you going to accidentally slip back
    into her womb?
Let your father's death end your fear.

OEDIPUS: It does it does.
Now I can find the end of this scourge.

JOCASTA: Come my lord,
No more questioning.
Your sympathy caused enough pain.
Let the sickness run its course,
We are not affected.

THE CARRIER: It is said your sickness is caused because
   you harbor your strong former King Laius' murderer.

JOCASTA: Let's to bed Oedipus.

OEDIPUS: That is what is said Carrier.
It was also said I would kill my father,
And bed my mother.

THE CARRIER:
Well don't fear bedding your mother my lord.

OEDIPUS: Why?

THE CARRIER: Because the woman who raised you,
Is not your mother!

JOCASTA & OEDIPUS: What?

THE CARRIER: Yes. Nothing to fear.
The people who raised you are not your parents.
They loved you like parents,
But produced no natural offspring.
I found you Oedipus, as a baby.
A slave was wandering the hills with you in infant
   state,
Knocking on peasant hut after peasant hut
Looking for a watcher.
The King and Queen wanted a son to raise,
To inherit what they could pass,
So I took you from the slave,
And gave you to Polybus.
It was his dying wish for me to tell you.
I guess I am just full of good news!

OEDIPUS: Do you hear this Jocasta?

JOCASTA: I do my lord.

(SICK MAN *again coughs a little.* NURSES *tend to him.*)

OEDIPUS:
Have you seen the slave that bore me since traveler?

THE CARRIER:
No, but he wore the brand of Laius' house.

OEDIPUS: Madame, comment you on this?

JOCASTA: This doesn't matter.
Seek nothing any more.
Let's go inside and shut the doors.
And question the world no more.
It doesn't matter.
This will end in ruin.
The answers will be ruin.
The truth is not the truth to know.
We are happy, my husband,
Are we not?
Why must we ruin this?
Ruin ruin ruin.
Why?
I have already lost one husband.
And my newborn baby...
No more loss can I handle.
Seek no more.
Let's go inside.
Come my husband, come!

OEDIPUS: I will wait for the slave we sent for.

JOCASTA: Why do you want to ruin us?

OEDIPUS: If we are ruined,
We have been ruined from my birth.

JOCASTA: Come inside, or you will meet the only truth
    there is: Death.

OEDIPUS: I will meet it.

JOCASTA: That was my last word.
My silence,
Long and heavy,
Will be my next plea.
(She exits.)

THE CARRIER: Why so quiet sir?
I feel that an eruption will spring from this silence.

OEDIPUS: Let it erupt.
I need to know who I am.
Fortune has blessed me for so long.
But who has fortune been blessing?
Not me but another.
Who wore my skin,
My name,
My shame,
Slept with my lovers,
Ate my food,
Another that owned my thoughts more than I.
I am not he.
But he is I.
And who is he,
Who is he?
And who am I?

THE CARRIER: I don't know man, I don't know.

OEDIPUS: You hungry?

THE CARRIER: A little sir

OEDIPUS: Come with me.
I will feed you.

THE CARRIER: Thank you.

(Exit OEDIPUS *and* THE CARRIER.*)*

(Enter JOCASTA. *The* SICK MAN *stands from the bed and watches* JOCASTA.*)*

JOCASTA: I know you.

SICK WOMAN: Yes, you do.

*(*JOCASTA *climbs into bathtub. The* NURSES *sing.)*

[The Song Of Jocasta's Desire]

*(*JOCASTA *slits her wrists, she dies.)*

SICK MAN: Oedipus, come forth.

(Enter OEDIPUS and THE CARRIER.)

OEDIPUS: Have you found the slave we sought?

SICK MAN: I am he.

OEDIPUS: Were you a slave in the house of Laius?

SICK MAN: Yes, Oedipus, I was slave to Laius.

THE CARRIER:
My lord this is the woman who gave me the child.

OEDIPUS: This woman?
You are her too?

THE CARRIER: Woman, do you remember wandering
    the hills with a bleeding child
And giving this charge to a stranger?
This King that stands before you is the child.

SICK MAN: I know it.
But with those words,
You have released a plague,
With a worse yoke than we suffer under now.

OEDIPUS: Did you give this Carrier a child?

SICK MAN: Yes, and I wish my own life too.

OEDIPUS: Where did this child come from,
Was it yours?

SICK MAN: It was not mine.

OEDIPUS: Who birthed the child?
Please, I need to know.

SICK MAN: You know.

OEDIPUS: Say it.

SICK MAN: Jocasta gave the child life.
From Laius.
Laius bid me kill it,
For fearing the fate of the babe.

OEDIPUS: What fate?

SICK MAN:
It was said that the baby would grow into a monster.
That will murder his father
And breed with his mother.

OEDIPUS: Then why did you not kill this baby.

SICK MAN: I pitied you.
Who could not pity an innocent child?
The clean skin,
The smell?
It is against our nature to ruin such purity.

OEDIPUS: If I gave you a child,
And told you it's life course,
The cruel and pitiless course of its life,
The wave of mutilation it will cause,
And I begged you to destroy him,
What would you do?
Knowing what you do now,
Tell me, would you destroy him?

SICK MAN: No sir.
Faced with that choice again,
I would take my own life.

OEDIPUS: Thank you.

SICK WOMAN: For what?

OEDIPUS: The truth…
Are you well enough to go?

SICK MAN: No, but I should not stay.

OEDIPUS: Then go.

SICK MAN: I'm sorry.

THE CARRIER:
But hold sir, there still is more suffering to behold.

(*Exit* SICK WOMAN.)

OEDIPUS: Is more suffering possible?

THE CARRIER: Yes.

(DEAD JOCASTA *rises and stares at* OEDIPUS. *Enter* CREON. *The* NURSES *sing.)*

(Underscoring the dialogue:

[The Violent Solemn Song]

OEDIPUS: No

THE CARRIER: By her own hand.
Her mind imagined that child,
The son,
That murdered the father.
The son that bred with the mother,
And gave birth to monstrous progeny.
Where she conceived a double brood of confused genetics,
Husband by a husband,
Children by a child.

(DEAD JOCASTA *exits to the underworld,* THE CARRIER *follows.)*

OEDIPUS: Oh my wife!
No, not wife- a teeming womb that bore me a twofold harvest,
Me and my children.
To see. To see.
No more to see,
The sights of woe, that I do know.
Drown me in darkness, to know no more,
What cruel life has in store.
To see no more!
No more no more!

(OEDIPUS *rips out his own eyes. The world goes dark.* CREON *enters.)*

OEDIPUS: Who looks upon this wretch?

CREON: I Creon.

OEDIPUS: Oh uncle brother,
I have wettened the womb from which I crawled.
I have drained the blood that sated my veins.
I must leave this land and laden this pox upon me.
Your sister, my brother,
My strong King uncle brother,
She is dead.

CREON: I see.

OEDIPUS: Point me to the gates,
To the dry wasteland,
Uncle brother keeper,
And shove me gone.
Do not pity me.

CREON: How can one hewn of human fabric not?
But I wait upon your daughters.
Here they come.

(Enter ANTIGONE and ISMENE, ISMENE whimpers.)

OEDIPUS: Can it be my pretty girls?
Antigone.
Ismene.
Is that you crying ?
Has Creon been benevolent enough to send me my
    darlings to kiss me bye?

ANTIGONE: 'Tis true father,
Brother,
Uncle,
Son,
King.
We are here.

OEDIPUS: O Creon, I beg you,
Please father these minnows,
For their natural parents,
The double mother and father brother, are gone.

Pity their youth, their innocence,
Let them know some sliver of happiness.

CREON: Oedipus,
I can do what I can do,
I am only human.

(Thunder)

CREON: The sky grows angry.
Time to pass.
The wasteland calls.

OEDIPUS: I must obey.

(Enter ETEOKLES *and* POLYNEICES *they stand by* CREON,
shocked by what they see.)

OEDIPUS: My sons, my heirs?
Is that you?
Polyneices, Eteokles?

CREON: They aren't here, Oedipus.

OEDIPUS: Oh.
May the reign of my brother-boys be better blest than
   mine.

CREON: How could it not?

ANTIGONE: We'll see.

OEDIPUS: I go, point me hence, I am willing.
Creon, tell my boys to take care of their sisters.

CREON: Oedipus, you must be confused,
Your daughters must go with you.

OEDIPUS: No, no no.

CREON:
Yes, you must take your unsprung offspring with you.
We truly cannot house them.
They are the waning wombs of the dissonant disease,
The mother bug egg sac freaks of congenital ruin and
   misery.

They must go,
They confuse the land,
Along with you.

OEDIPUS: Don't do this,
Let me go alone.

CREON: Order me not.
Take your unloved skinny chickens with you.

OEDIPUS: Boys, my boys help me.
Children help me
Where are you, boys?

(ETEOKLES *exits, smiling.* POLYNEICES *stares.*)

ANTIGONE: Your girls are here, father.
Ismene clear the way ahead.

(ISMENE *exits.* ANTIGONE *helps* OEDIPUS *to his feet.*)

CREON: Go, you infected derelict, the wasteland calls,
And Thebes longs to breathe clean air.

OEDIPUS: I am so sorry.

CREON: Go!

(*Thunder. Exit* OEDIPUS *led by* ANTIGONE. *Exit*
POLYNEICES *followed by* CREON, *the sky brightens.*)

(*The* NURSES *try to clean the blood left behind by* OEDIPUS.)

NEW NURSE: These are long days.

NURSE: They just get longer.

END OF ACT 1

ACT 2: IN TRACHIS

(The NURSES *are cleaning. Enter* DEJANIRA.*)*

DEJANIRA: Have you seen my husband?
No normal man.
Herakles his name.
Have you seen him?

NURSE: No.

DEJANIRA: Well you would know it if you saw him.
I am Dejanira, his wife
You know me?

NURSE: We know you ma'am.

DEJANIRA: They say,
You don't know whether life is sweet or bitter until it's
   over.
But I know, my life is bitter.
Maybe that means it's over.

NURSE: No.

DEJANIRA: Herakles fought off all my wooers,
Like he were fighting a cold.
It was nice, for a while.
He leaves, and long, long goes the time till he returns.
I wait.
Night upon night,
Month upon month,
Wait wait wait.
Knowing either the sickness or adolescent lust burns

him.
But still I give him my love,
And bore him a son.
Hyllus, you know him?

NURSE: We know him.

DEJANIRA: He's cute, right.

NURSE: Sure, Dejanira.
He's cute.

DEJANIRA: Hyllus is not like his dad.
He's sensitive, delicate.
Not like his dad.
His dad is steel,
And he's gold.
I can never let him be like his dad.
All the time, "Mom let me go on labors."
I always give him some task to do around the house to make him feel strong.
He's a feminine young man, my baby.

(HYLLUS *bursts through the doors, with a lot of boyish energy.*)

HYLLUS: I have a surprise for you.

DEJANIRA: Hyllus, son, what are you doing?

HYLLUS: I know where Father is.

DEJANIRA:
Oh baby, don't ask to go looking for him again.
Don't break your mother's heart by leaving.
You stay here with me, your father will come home someday…

HYLLUS: Yes, soon,
I heard them talking.

DEJANIRA: About what?

HYLLUS: They say he's just about to end a war with the
  City of the Barren Hills.

DEJANIRA: Where?

HYLLUS: The City of the Barren Hills.

DEJANIRA: Oh no.

HYLLUS: What?

DEJANIRA: Why would he want to conquer The City of
the Barren Hills?
They have nothing of value,
Just barren hills.

HYLLUS: I don't know.

DEJANIRA: That city rages with contagion.

HYLLUS: Okay.

DEJANIRA: An Oracle said, If he destroys The City of
the Barren Hills,
He will bring home a virus that will infect us all,
And bring his death.

HYLLUS: What virus?

DEJANIRA: I don't know.
Hyllus, son,
You must go to him.

HYLLUS: What?
Really?

DEJANIRA: Yes,
Flee,
Fly as fast as you can,
Fly.
Go.

HYLLUS: When?

DEJANIRA: Now.
I'm letting you free to be a man.

HYLLUS: What do I pack?

DEJANIRA: Nothing,
Go, stop Herakles from claiming The City of the Barren
  Hills.

HYLLUS: Yes.
Okay.
I love you mom.

DEJANIRA: Go!

(HYLLUS *exits.*)

DEJANIRA: I lost him,
I lost my husband.
I am widow to the proudest of proud-men.

NURSE: You haven't lost him.

NEW NURSE: Yet.

(THE CARRIER *enters.*)

THE CARRIER: Is this Dejanira?

NURSE: Yes.

DEJANIRA: Who are you?

THE CARRIER: A Carrier ma'am.

DEJANIRA: Oh no no, he's dead.
He's dead.

THE CARRIER: Who's dead?

DEJANIRA: Herakles.

THE CARRIER: No, he's not dead.
He's home.

DEJANIRA: Home?
So soon?

THE CARRIER: Yes, this night he will sup at your table.

DEJANIRA: In defeat, right?

THE CARRIER: Why would you hope for the impossible?
Herakles in defeat, we'll all die first.

DEJANIRA: Who reports his victory?

THE CARRIER:
Philoktetes, Herakles' friend, is proclaiming to all.
He ran ahead of Herakles and the rest of the troops.
Pushing through swarms of sick people crowded
   around,
To hear any optimism they can gather,
From the Story of Herakles' Victory Against The City
   of the Barren Hills.

NURSE: Does Herakles show any signs of weakness?

THE CARRIER: Herakles weak?
No way.

DEJANIRA: Does he bring back a sickness?

THE CARRIER: From what I hear,
He is as healthy as when he left.
The only thing he brings back are the spoils of war.

DEJANIRA: What spoils?

(*Enter* PHILOKTETES.)

PHILOKTETES:
Dejanira, wife to Herakles, how lovely you look.

DEJANIRA: Hello Philoktetes, Philoktetes.
Welcome, welcome.

PHILOKTETES: I am so happy to be home,
This one was far too long.
Herakles, will be here shortly,
He is speaking with the poor, sick families of our fallen
soldiers to pass on his respects.
Excuse me my lady,
I must prepare something for my lord.

(PHILOKTETES *exits for a second and returns with a very
intriguing young woman,* IOLE. PHILOKTETES *tries to escort*
IOLE *somewhere.*)

DEJANIRA: Who is this girl, Philoktetes?

PHILOKTETES:
A captive from the City of the Barren Hills.

DEJANIRA: A common captive?

PHILOKTETES: Yes, I think so.

DEJANIRA: Why would he sack this empty city?

PHILOKTETES: Who knows.
Whim?

DEJANIRA: And this girl?

PHILOKTETES: What about her?

DEJANIRA: I get thickened with compassion, seeing her.
To live as a slave now over Herakles' whim.
Such an unhealthy life for such a healthy girl.

PHILOKTETES: Yes ma'am.

DEJANIRA: Girl, who are you?
A maid, a mother?
She looks at me with such, such, I can't say…
It's pity. As if she pities me.
Do you pity me?

IOLE: Yes.
I pity you.

DEJANIRA: Why?
Why?
Philoktetes, whose child is she?

PHILOKTETES: I don't know.
She is no more special than the others.

DEJANIRA: Is she of royalty?

PHILOKTETES: I don't know, I didn't ask.

DEJANIRA: What is she called?

PHILOKTETES:
I was not allowed to speak with her, Dejanira.
Excuse me, I should bring this girl to her quarters?

DEJANIRA: Her quarters?

PHILOKTETES: Yes ma'am.

DEJANIRA: Here?

PHILOKTETES: Yes ma'am.

DEJANIRA:
Unshaken girl, why aren't you with the other captives?
Confidence hangs about you like flies on carrion.
Why?
Who are you?

IOLE: My name is Iole.

DEJANIRA: Why are you here?
What do you have in your hand?

(IOLE *reveals an apple.*)

IOLE: A apple.

PHILOKTETES: We must go Dejanira.
Excuse us.

(PHILOKTETES *exits with the* IOLE.)

DEJANIRA: What is going on?

NURSE: I don't know.

THE CARRIER: My lady, forgive me for saying so,
But Philoktetes just lied to you.

DEJANIRA: What?

THE CARRIER: I heard Philoktetes say,
In the throngs of others,
That it was for that girl's sake Herakles destroyed the
City of the Barren Hills.
He requested her company from her father the King.
And when his request was denied,
Well, as always,
Herakles got what he wanted.

DEJANIRA: And he means to keep this girl?

THE CARRIER: I assume so.
I don't think he'd sack a city for a girl,
Then just leave her to wander the woods.

DEJANIRA: You knew this all along?

THE CARRIER: I felt it was not my job to tell you,
Yet I could not see your torment prolonged.

DEJANIRA: This girl is the infection foretold.

(Enter PHILOKTETES.)

PHILOKTETES: I must go to Herakles.
Do you need anything before I go?

DEJANIRA: The truth, Philoktetes.

PHILOKTETES: In what regard?

DEJANIRA: Who is that girl?

PHILOKTETES: I don't know, other than she is from the
City of the Barren Hills.

THE CARRIER: Sir, have you no shame?

PHILOKTETES: And you, do you know your place?

THE CARRIER: Answer your lady: who have you
brought into her home?

PHILOKTETES: A common captive maiden.
Who is this person?

THE CARRIER: Captive, yes,
But common, no.
Tell your lady who the fair one is.

PHILOKTETES: Who is she stranger?

THE CARRIER:
Tell her the girl is Herakles' new won bride.

PHILOKTETES: Who said this?
Dejanira, don't listen to this fool.

THE CARRIER:
You announced it yourself, proudly in the street.

Trying to give hope to the sad masses.
You said for in her skin lives a new day for this city.
Her purity shall release us from troubles.

PHILOKTETES: That's a good story.

DEJANIRA: Please excuse us Carrier.
Thank you.

THE CARRIER: For sure.
(Exits)

DEJANIRA: Philoktetes, do not starve me of truth.
Am I to be cast aside?
Why should he not be consumed by her beauty?
While my age is a growing obstacle, her age is
    enhancement.
Philoktetes, give compassion to a former beauty, still
    your lady.
Please.

PHILOKTETES: Compassion, what about some for me?
When Herakles finds out...
The truth. Yes.
Herakles wanted that girl.
So smitten with lust did he desolate The City of the
Barren Hills.
But, Dejanira, should I have said that to you,
Should have I said,
"Hey lady, this fox is your husband's new young bride.
Go make her some supper. She likes souvlaki."
Where would have that led us?
I don't want to hurt you Dejanira.
I grieve Herakles has done this to you.
But that is the truth you wanted.
You have been replaced,
Like old batteries.

DEJANIRA: Yes, well...
No matter how violently the heart beats,

It should be met with love.
Love, right?

PHILOKTETES: I guess.

DEJANIRA: I will meet Herakles with love,
A gift of love.
It's time, right?

PHILOKTETES: I don't know.
What time, ma'am?

DEJANIRA: Please give my husband this gift for me.
(She gets box from some hidden place.)
It's a robe.

*(DEJANIRA opens the box and takes out the contents to show
PHILOKTETES. It is indeed a robe, and not a very nice one
either.)*

PHILOKTETES: Oooh, a robe.

(DEJANIRA then packs the robe back in the box and seals it.)

DEJANIRA: But please, as you have been loyal to me,
Do not let anyone else wear this robe.
It must not see the light of day until Herakles wears it.

PHILOKTETES: My lady, thank you.
He's going to love this robe.

DEJANIRA:
Now, I will go and welcome my husband's new bride.

PHILOKTETES: It makes me happy to hear you say that.
I am sorry that things turned out this way.
It won't be as bad as one might think.

(PHILOKTETES kisses DEJANIRA on the cheek.)

DEJANIRA: Maybe not Philoktetes,
Maybe not.
Go, thank you.

(PHILOKTETES exits.)

NURSE: Are you alright?

DEJANIRA: No, not really.
For this young maiden…
No, not a maiden, but a mistress.
No, more than a mistress,
For I am the mistress,
Or the maid,
And she is his wife.
His love.
She has infected my house.

(Enter IOLE.*)*

IOLE: Excuse me...

DEJANIRA: Yes, sugarplum?

IOLE: I was wondering if you could tell me where the
bathroom is.
I tried to hold it.
But I drank all this juice.

DEJANIRA: Through there.

IOLE: Thank you.

DEJANIRA: Are you settled?

IOLE: Yes, ma'am.
I didn't have a chance to bring much,
But what I did bring, is away.

DEJANIRA: Where did Philoktetes put you?

IOLE: The big bed room.

DEJANIRA: The pink one?

IOLE: It's pink, yes.
Excuse me.

DEJANIRA:
Maybe you expect me to cede my marriage bed?
Explain how he likes his things—
Like his food,
Like his sex.

IOLE: No, ma'am.
I'm sorry, excuse me.

DEJANIRA: You really are pretty.

IOLE: Thank you.

DEJANIRA: So pretty.
Look at those cheeks.
Look at all... that.
The flower of your visage blooms while mine withers.
Oh I hate you.

IOLE: The bathroom is through here?

DEJANIRA: I'm sorry.
La la la.
We don't need to worry.
Right?

IOLE: No ma'am?

DEJANIRA:
No, because we'll be moving you out of that room,
Soon, right?

IOLE: I'm sorry ma'am, he was real clear about it.

DEJANIRA: I'm sure he was,
But that was before.

IOLE: Before what?

DEJANIRA: Before I gave my husband a gift.
I gave him a robe, okay.
To make him love me.

IOLE: A robe?
A robe will convince him to love you?

DEJANIRA: Yes.

NURSE: That must be some robe.

DEJANIRA: It's charmed.
Like me.

IOLE: You're charmed?

DEJANIRA: When I was a girl,
Like your age,
Maybe even much younger,
Maybe even much prettier,
I would visit a river.
There lived an ancient creature,
A horse as much as a man.
So grotesque, but gentle.
One day, I asked this beast for a ride 'cross the river.
Herakles, stumbling on this scene,
Thinking I was in danger,
Shot an arrow from his Golden Bow.
The Man-Horse, fell, dying,
And told me that this fatal archer, Herakles, will be my
    husband,
And would love me for a long time.
But one day my husband's love will be wrapped
    around another,
Like blood congealing over a wound.
Then the Horse-Man said,
In his equine semen lived a chemical,
That would keep Herakles faithful to me,
Activated by sunlight.
So I...harvested some of his dying semen,
(No small task for a small girl)
And kept it in a light tight jar.
With this ancient potent seed,
I doused that robe,
And kept it for this very day.
Once Herakles wears that robe,
And the sun shines upon it,
Thoughts of you,
You adorable child-girl,
Will be ejaculated from his mind.
And I will hold his heart again.

For you see,
I have not the patience to grow old,
While you more ripe.
See?

NURSE: No way will this turn out well.

IOLE: Excuse me,
I really have to go.

DEJANIRA: Then go.
We'll find you a nice place to live.

(DEJANIRA *guides* IOLE *though the door to exit. The sun shines outside.* DEJANIRA *suddenly grabs her hand in great agitation.*)

DEJANIRA: Ahh.

NURSE: What happened?

DEJANIRA: I don't know yet.

NURSE: What is it?

(*The* NURSES *try to help her.*)

DEJANIRA: Oh, It burns, burns.

NURSE: Let us see it.

DEJANIRA: Something, was...I think I need to sit down.

NURSE: What's wrong with your hand?

DEJANIRA: It's burns, I can't stand it.

NURSE: What happened?

DEJANIRA: This hand touched the robe.
The sun just shone across it.
Oh no, I think I may have made a mistake.

NURSE: What?

(DEJANIRA *holds out a melted, bloody hand.*)

NURSE: Oh mercy.

DEJANIRA:
I think I have done some terrible terrible thing
I don't know, I don't know.
Why would the monster, dying, show me good will?
I am infected with trust.
I infect people with trust.
This trust brings destruction.
No more to trust,
No more to trust.

NURSE: Sit still.

DEJANIRA:
There is no room for hope in the face of such decay.

NURSE: It's just cinders and some jellied bone.
I have never seen anything like this.

NURSE: Do you need something for the pain?

DEJANIRA: Yes, but nothing you can give.

(Enter HYLLUS *with a knife.)*

HYLLUS:
Sinful, vindictive horror-mare of jealous doom!

DEJANIRA: Hello son.

HYLLUS: You have given him your "gift",
And he got your "message",
And his message will be returned by me.
Are you ready to meet your death?

DEJANIRA: Don't speak.
Sshh.
Just do it.

*(*DEJANIRA *kneels before* HYLLUS, *who holds the knife to her heart.)*

DEJANIRA: It's okay baby,
You can do it.

*(*HYLLUS *backs away.)*

HYLLUS: I can't.
I am too soft.

NURSE: What happened to Herakles?

HYLLUS: The robe happened to Herakles.
We first noticed the smell,
Like meat left too long on a spit.
In the sunlight,
The red robe radiated,
Like isotopic destruction.
It fused with his skin,
Until the threshold was lost twixt the blistering flesh
    and burning fabric.
But still the vicious venom sank deeper to decimate
    muscle.
Philoktetes covered him with clothes and submerged
    him in a water trough.
But too little, too late, barely a piece of skin stayed on
    his yellow frame.
The tenacious poison continues to corrode deeper and
    deeper, to his organs.
Who knows when and if his death will come?
And who knows when and if the pain will stop?
Philoktetes began dragging him here.
I ran ahead to present my gift,
Of your dead body,
To his decaying one.

DEJANIRA: Yes, please get the strength to kill me.
But know this my lovely boy,
I was lied to,
I didn't mean it.

HYLLUS: What?

DEJANIRA: I was given a potion to make him love me.
But there was no love in that potion,
Like my life now.
It was stupidity, not malice.

I wanted him to love me.
Forever.
And my crime was that I believed he would.

HYLLUS: What?

DEJANIRA: Yes my son.
Now kill me out of love, not hate.

HYLLUS: I can't.

DEJANIRA: I know.

(NURSES *sing.*)

[The Song Of Dejanira's Trust]

(DEJANIRA *drinks the bleach and kills herself.*)

NURSE: The last labor of Herakles.

(*Enter* PHILOKTETES *bursts through the door, dragging the very bloody and skinless* HERAKLES *followed by the* CARRIER. *The* NURSES *try to tend to* HERAKLES, *but he is writhing in pain.*)

HERAKLES: What where am I?
Who are these enemies?
What parasite is digesting me?

(HERAKLES *pushes away the* NURSES)

PHILOKTETES: They try to ease your suffering Herakles.

HERAKLES: There is no easy suffering, Philoktetes.

HYLLUS: Calm down Father.

HERAKLES: Stop whining, son.

HYLLUS: I can't.

HERAKLES: Ahh, the acid swells again.

PHILOKTETES: Let these maidens ease your pain.

NURSE:
Philoktetes, there is actually nothing we can do.

HERAKLES: My labors were lies,
Fantasies that lead me to this awful pain.
Even the seven-headed dog was more inviting than my
    cruel wife.
She sewn this nest of fury to my skin,
Scrubbed red my flesh.
I am a captive in unshakeable shackles.
No giant, or dragon, or water spirit did this to me,
But a woman.
The Oracles said I would be killed by a dead man, not
    a woman.
I can get through this.
Son, bring me your mother.

HYLLUS: You won't punish her.

HERAKLES: Yes I will.

HYLLUS: I can't bring her to you.

HERAKLES: How could you disobey me?

THE CARRIER: He doesn't disobey you,
She can't be retrieved.
She is dead.

(DEAD DEJANIRA *stands and stares at* HERAKLES.)

HERAKLES: By whom?

THE CARRIER: Herself.
Her guilt.
Her lost youth,
And lost love.

HERAKLES: She should have died by me.

HYLLUS: She faltered, but not from malice,
But from love and innocence.

HERAKLES: Is this then love dissolving my flesh?

HYLLUS: No, but she thought it was a charm,
To take your eye from your new bride and see her
    again as she was in youth.

NEW NURSE: The charm was given to her by the Horse-
Man you killed.

HERAKLES: The Horse-Man?

NURSE: Yes.

HERAKLES: So, this is the work of a dead man.
And this will mean my death.

HYLLUS: It was not mother's fault.

HERAKLES:
No, the woman was infected with lies, like we all are.
Bury her with love son.

(DEAD DEJANIRA *exits to the underworld.*)

HERAKLES: Give me your hand, son.

HYLLUS: Why?

HERAKLES: Just do what I say.

(HYLLUS *holds the hand of* HERAKLES. HERAKLES *pulls him
really close and gives him a bear hug.*)

HERAKLES: Hold me tight.

HYLLUS: I am.

HERAKLES: Tighter.

HYLLUS (*Trying to hold as tight as he can*) Arr.

HERAKLES: You smell like a woman.

(HERAKLES *pushes* HYLLUS *away.*)

HYLLUS: I'm sorry.

HERAKLES: Swear to honor me.

HYLLUS: Okay.

HERAKLES: Swear it.

HYLLUS: I do. I swear it.

HERAKLES: And if you break this oath,
Never shall this land find peace,

Until all succumb to a sickness-death.

HYLLUS: I swear.

HERAKLES: I need you to get the incinerator ready.

HYLLUS: Are you cold?

HERAKLES: No, I need you to cremate my body.

PHILOKTETES: Herakles, come on.

HERAKLES: What?

PHILOKTETES: Don't ask your son to burn you alive.

HERAKLES: This is not your business Philoktetes.
Son, you must do this, and do not mourn me.
If you cry, you betray my name.
Then this land is cursed forever.

HYLLUS: You want me to become your murderer?

HERAKLES: No, my healer.
Cure me of this body.
Of this hatred.
Of the lies I have lived.
Let me go to the underworld.
Please help me.

HYLLUS: By burning you in a fire?

HERAKLES: Yes. Son, please.
I have lost my strength.
What is Herakles without strength?
A story, a lie.
Please Hyllus.

HYLLUS: Okay.

PHILOKTETES: Herakles.

HYLLUS: You can help by getting the incinerator ready,
    Philoktetes.

PHILOKTETES: This is madness.
(He unlocks the incinerator.)

HERAKLES: Bring me my Golden Bow.
I will make a gift of my Golden Bow, son,
When you light the pyre.

HYLLUS: Thank you.

HERAKLES: And bring forth the girl I returned with.

(THE CARRIER *exits.*)

HYLLUS: What do you want with the girl?

HERAKLES: She, like my Golden Bow, is yours now.

HYLLUS: No, I can't marry her.
She drove my mother's fatal hand.

HERAKLES: She is only a girl, don't blame her.

HYLLUS: I can't marry her.

HERAKLES: Son, it's only right.
Her homeland is destroyed,
Please, fulfill my promise to her of a better life.

(*Enter* IOLE.)

IOLE: Herakles.

HERAKLES: I know I am gross.
Go to Hyllus,
He is your husband now.

IOLE: Him?
The boy?

HYLLUS: Wait outside, I'll explain later.

(IOLE *exits. Enter the* CARRIER *with the Golden Bow.*)

THE CARRIER: The Golden Bow of Herakles.

HERAKLES: Thank you,
Give it to Hyllus.

(THE CARRIER *gives* HYLLUS *the Golden Bow.*)

THE CARRIER: Be careful with this.
(*He exits.*)

PHILOKTETES: It's ready.
Your death-chamber is ready.

HERAKLES: I have been jilted by might,
And impotency courts me,
Keep my Golden Bow, son,
And the world will know,
Your sturdy hand
Mercifully smothered the inglorious man,
Herakles unhinged.

(HYLLUS *drops the Golden Bow.*)

PHILOKTETES: What are you doing Hyllus?

HYLLUS: I can't.

HERAKLES:
Come, son, cauterize my soul from this corrosion.

HYLLUS: No, sir.
I'm not that man,
I am not the man you want me to be.

PHILOKTETES: You gave him your oath.

HYLLUS: I guess my oath was a lie, like his life.
We can't see the truth of the future;
The truth of the past is perverted
By fabricated remembrances.
Only in the present can we see the truth.
And this truth, is not for me.
I will marry this girl though.
(He exits.)

HERAKLES: Help me son.
Fulfill your oath!
Why do you forsake me?

PHILOKTETES: He is gone.

HERAKLES:
Do not mourn my death, but my loss of honor.
Even in death my labors bear no merit.

Take my Golden Bow Philoktetes,
For only you honor me.

(PHILOKTETES *takes the Golden Bow and* HERAKLES *goes into the incinerator.*)

PHILOKTETES: Be still and wait for death.
For it will not come quickly.

HERAKLES: This is the end,
The end of Herakles.
The end of the lies I have lead.
To those I harmed out of misguided pride-lust,
Say I am sorry.

PHILOKTETES: Now be still.
No more lust.
No more lies.
Let it go.

(PHILOKTETES *ignites the incinerator and watches* HERAKLES *scream and burn, like he is watching a campfire. When the screams of* HERAKLES *die down,* PHILOKTETES *exits with the Golden Bow.*)

(NEW NURSE *stops the incinerator and opens the door. Smoke fills the space. She dumps a bucket of water inside.*)

NEW NURSE: I don't want to do this any more.

NURSE: What else are we going to do?
Help me clean.

END OF ACT 2

ACT 3: IN COLONUS

(The NURSES *are cleaning.)*

*(*ANTIGONE *enters, screaming. She looks a mess, she is cut and bruised and dirty, her face is covered from the sun. She is dragging* OEDIPUS *on a sheet or with a rope, his clothes are tattered and dirty, his eye-holes are bandaged and bloody, his face is covered.)*

ANTIGONE: Help me!
Help!

NURSE: What is it?

ANTIGONE: It's my father,
Help.

NEW NURSE: How long has he been like this?

ANTIGONE: Since this morning.

NURSE: How long have you been in the desert?

ANTIGONE: Ten years.

NEW NURSE: What happened to his eyes?

ANTIGONE: This is the fallen king of Thebes.
Oedipus.

(The NURSES *sit* OEDIPUS *on the hospital bed, and try to help him.* THESEUS *enters with a bucket of flowers.)*

THESEUS: Oh no, no no.
You can't leave Oedipus here.

NURSE: This man is very ill.

THESEUS: We can't have him rest here.

ANTIGONE: This place is a trash heap,
Let these women tend to him.

THESEUS: This place is no trash heap, it's our city.

ANTIGONE: Where are we?

THESEUS: Colonus, ruled by Athenian law,
That dictates, any infected trespassers,
Will be met with corporeal punishment.

NEW NURSE:
Corporeally, I don't think he could get much worse.

(OEDIPUS *jolts awake.*)

OEDIPUS: Antigone! Where are you?

ANTIGONE: I'm here father.

OEDIPUS: Where are we?

ANTIGONE: Colonus.

OEDIPUS: Ah, my birthplace.

ANTIGONE: No, you were born in Thebes.

OEDIPUS: What's that smell?

ANTIGONE: It's you, father.

OEDIPUS: No, over that.

ANTIGONE: I don't know.

OEDIPUS: Is it flowers?

ANTIGONE: Yes, I thought they were fake.

THESEUS: No, they're real.

OEDIPUS: Who's that?

ANTIGONE: Some jerk off.

OEDIPUS: Does he help me?

ANTIGONE: No.

OEDIPUS: Can I see your king, please, sir.

THESEUS: I need you to leave.

OEDIPUS: I need you to bring me your king.

THESEUS: No sir, I'm sorry, not until you leave.

ANTIGONE: Who's your king?

THESEUS: Theseus.

ANTIGONE: Get Theseus here,
Tell him King Oedipus calls.
Go idiot!

NURSE: Antigone, this is Theseus.

ANTIGONE: *(Kneeling)*
Excuse me, your highness.

THESEUS: It's alright, how would you know?

ANTIGONE: Can my father please stay?

THESEUS: No.

OEDIPUS: Please Theseus,
I just want to rest,
In peace.

THESEUS: I want that to,
But you can't here.
This is my city,
It needs to remain pure if we have any hope of
   salvation.
And you might be infected with the disease you left
   festering in Thebes.
We can't take chance, sir.

OEDIPUS: In the past ten years,
I asked no man, for no favor.
Now I ask you one favor.
Let me please sit among those flowers.

NURSE: Theseus.

THESEUS: What?

NEW NURSE: What's the harm?

THESEUS: I don't know yet.
Let me speak to my advisors.
(He exits.)

ANTIGONE: He's kind of tense.

NURSE: Yeah, he's good at his job.

(Enter CREON.)

CREON: It's been a while child?

OEDIPUS: Who comes?

ANTIGONE: You wouldn't believe it if I told you.

CREON: You grew.

ANTIGONE: I guess, Creon.

CREON: Don't be scared, I bear no ill will.
I am old, and hope to be older still.

OEDIPUS: Creon, why are you here?

CREON: Because of you, Oedipus.

OEDIPUS: How did you find me?

CREON: The Blind Seer told me.
How are you?

OEDIPUS: Do I not look well?

CREON: Oedipus, I come to humble myself.
To ask for forgiveness.

OEDIPUS: Forgiveness?

CREON: Yes, Oedipus.
I was wrong.
Thebes suffers, your sons make Thebes suffer.
I came here to ask you a favor.
Don't make Thebes crumble for my mistakes.

OEDIPUS: What could I possibly do?

CREON: Rule the Theban Throne.
Wear the crown, care for the people again.

OEDIPUS: Rule the Theban Throne?

CREON: Yes sir, be our king again, please.

OEDIPUS: Do you hear this, Antigone?

ANTIGONE: I hear him, yes.

CREON: Time has shown me my errors.
Be my king again, please.
The people of Thebes call for you every day.
Your rule was just, compassionate.
Your sons are haughty, drunken brawlers.
We suffer under their rule.
Please, Our Strong Former King, come home with me.

OEDIPUS: Am I valued now?
As a man?
Valued.

CREON: Yes, Oedipus, take your rightful place on the
Theban Throne.

OEDIPUS: Creon, give me a moment.

CREON: Of course.

OEDIPUS: What do you think Antigone?

ANTIGONE: Something doesn't seem right.

OEDIPUS: Why?

ANTIGONE: I don't trust it.

OEDIPUS: It's everything I want.
Forgiveness, respect, glory.

ANTIGONE: That's why I don't trust it.

OEDIPUS: Don't you think I deserve it?

ANTIGONE: I think you are a good man,
And deserve all that any man should have.
And you were robbed of so much in life.

But do you deserve to rule the Theban Throne again?
I don't think so, Father.

OEDIPUS: How dare you child?

ANTIGONE:
If Thebes wants you back sir, it is for no benefit to you.

OEDIPUS: After all these years, you betray me now.

ANTIGONE: No, how could you think that?

OEDIPUS: Why did you tend to me all those years,
If you had no faith in me.

ANTIGONE: I have faith in you,
As a man, not as king.

OEDIPUS: But I am a king Antigone.

ANTIGONE: No sir, you were one,
By an accident from a tempest-teamed line.

OEDIPUS: It was no accident.

ANTIGONE: Don't want this, let it go.

OEDIPUS: How can I forfeit all I have fought for?

ANTIGONE: If you want comfort, love, respect.
I give you all, more than faceless subjects can.
But if you want pride, then go, find it in the illusion of
   power.

OEDIPUS:
I would never have guessed you would discard me so.
You who loved me,
Who quenched me with your tears of sorrow.
Fed me your own flesh to stave starvation.
When others want me, I am useless to you.
I am going back to Thebes.

ANTIGONE:
Just ten minutes ago you couldn't even walk,
I had to drag you for miles.

OEDIPUS: I am sorry I was a burden to you.

ANTIGONE: Don't be blind.
You know Creon.
You know Thebes.
This is rotten.

OEDIPUS: I thought I knew you too,
But it seems my perceptions are delusions.
Creon.

CREON: Yes Oedipus.

OEDIPUS: The people want me?

CREON: They do sir, more than health,
Do they want to see Oedipus sit on the Theban Throne.

OEDIPUS: Then guide me home, Brother.

CREON: Oh noble Oedipus,
This will make Thebes blessed.

(CREON *guides* OEDIPUS *off the bed.*)

ANTIGONE: Father…

OEDIPUS: Stay here if you want child,
My country needs me.

NEW NURSE: He'll never make it.

ANTIGONE: I know.

(*Enter a drunken* POLYNEICES.)

POLYNEICES: Where are you two going?

(POLYNEICES *pushes* CREON. OEDIPUS *falls,* ANTIGONE
and the NURSES *help him on the bed.*)

CREON: Polyneices.

ANTIGONE: Brother!

POLYNEICES: What has this crook told you?

CREON: How did you find us?

POLYNEICES: The Blind Seer.

CREON: I thought she told just me.

POLYNEICES: Who can you trust anymore?

OEDIPUS: Is this my son?

POLYNEICES: Yes Father.

(POLYNEICES *hugs* OEDIPUS.)

OEDIPUS: What's that smell?

ANTIGONE: I think he's drunk father.

POLYNEICES: You want a drink, buddy?

OEDIPUS: Buddy?
No.
Why are you here?

POLYNEICES: To save you.

OEDIPUS: From what?

POLYNEICES: Creon.
Shhh.

CREON: Don't listen to him.

ANTIGONE: He wants Father to come back and rule the
    Theban Throne.

POLYNEICES: It's not Creon's throne to give.

OEDIPUS: You don't want me to come back and rule?

POLYNEICES: No.
Yes sir I do,
But not with Creon.
I want you to bless my throne Father.

CREON: What throne is that?
The one at the tavern?

POLYNEICES: The Theban Throne is mine.

CREON: Oedipus, the people ousted him,
Rightly installed his younger brother.

ANTIGONE: Eteokles is king?

POLYNEICES: Eteokles is a dick…tator.
A dictator.
He cares as much about the people
As Creon does Oedipus.
I was forced off the throne.

OEDIPUS: A rebellion?

POLYNEICES: Yes sir, a violent insurrection.

CREON: That's not true, it was a deal they made,
To exchange the throne annually,
But when it came time for Polyneices to rule.
He was off drunk in Bohemia,
With women of loose-convictions.
(He caught crabs.)
The people wanted to keep Eteokles in power.

ANTIGONE: If you're so fond of Eteokles,
Why are you trying to give his throne to Father?

CREON: It rightfully belongs to Oedipus.

POLYNEICES: And if not to Oedipus, then to me.

OEDIPUS: Do the Theban people want me back?

CREON & POLYNEICES: (Lying) Yes.

CREON: They want you as their king Oedipus.

POLYNEICES: They want you to bless my throne, sire.
You should live out your days as king,
Before I take the Theban Throne.

OEDIPUS: I want this to be true.

ANTIGONE: Father, you know it's not.

OEDIPUS: Can't I dream?

ANTIGONE: No, it's not healthy.

OEDIPUS: Then what do I believe in?

ANTIGONE: Just pain sir.

OEDIPUS: Yes, you're right.
I can't go Creon.

CREON: Oh sad, that's sad.
I didn't want it to come to this.

ANTIGONE: Come to what?

CREON: By order of Eteokles, rightful ruler of Thebes,
I order you, Oedipus to return to Thebes.

OEDIPUS: Order me? No.

CREON: Then I must take you by force.

ANTIGONE: Over my corpse will you do that.

CREON: That shouldn't be too difficult.

(CREON *approches* OEDIPUS, ANTIGONE *stops him*,
POLYNEICES *quickly fights with* CREON. *Enter* ISMENE,
exhausted.)

ISMENE: Father, father.

(ISMENE *collapses,* ANTIGONE *rushes to her.*)

ANTIGONE: Ismene.

ISMENE: *(Out of breath)*
Sister, I'm alright.
I came as fast as I can,
Tracking Polyneices.
He's fast.

POLYNEICES: Like lightning sis.

OEDIPUS: What's wrong, daughter?

ISMENE: Father, don't trust either of these men.
The Blind Seer came to both with an oracle he would
    share with no other.

OEDIPUS: What oracle?

ISMENE: I don't know the depth of the story, Father,
But Thebes lives in its darkest age.

The past ten years have been a stain upon honor and
    decency.

POLYNEICES: No stain of mine Father.

ANTIGONE: Let her finish.

POLYNEICES: Yes sir.

ISMENE: Upon your banishment,
Polyneices and Eteokles jointly gave Creon the throne,
To cure the city of the plague caused by our tainted
    blood,
The genetic ulcer that bled our bloodline.

CREON: I rejected the throne at first,
But relented for the good of Thebes.

POLYNEICES: The good of Creon.

ISMENE: As your boys grew,
So did their greedy desire.
And they reclaimed the throne from Creon.

CREON: As was their right.
And I abdicated happily.

POLYNEICES: To return to your life of riches and sloth.

ISMENE: That is when we got word,
Antigone and I could return to Thebes.
I returned, but as you know, Antigone remained to
comfort you.
Your sons made a pact...

POLYNEICES: To exchange the throne annually between
    us, like was said.

ISMENE: The first rule was of the younger, Eteokles,
And he ruled with a stormy temper.

POLYNEICES: Stormy is a little soft to describe him.
He's a dick...tator.
We discussed this.

ISMENE: And the illness in our people grew, not waned.
The year term expired, and instead of yielding,
Eteokles fixed himself to the throne,
And refused to submit to Polyneices.

POLYNEICES: Then upon crazed regality,
Eteokles, banished me.
Pushed me from Thebes.

ISMENE: So spited and spiteful, this banished boy,
Gathered six other war-like captains,
And swore to rip Eteokles off the throne.

POLYNEICES: *(Excited)* Yeah!

ISMENE: Or destroy the city.

POLYNEICES: *(Ashamed)* Ya.

CREON: The Seven Against Thebes they call themselves.

ISMENE: The Seven Against Thebes waits outside the
    Theban gates now,
Itching for Polyneices to give the order to attack.

OEDIPUS: Is this true?

CREON & POLYNEICES: Mostly.

OEDIPUS: What do you say Polyneices?

POLYNEICES: Look Father Brother,
I too have been banished from our home.
I haven't maintained as much dignity as you, my
    friend.

OEDIPUS: Dignity?

POLYNEICES: I guess, I don't know.
Look at me.

ANTIGONE: Polyneices.

POLYNEICES: Right.
I want the Theban Throne.
Eteokles keeps it.
He just locked me out.

Like he were my wife and I came home drunk too late
  one night.
I need you to return and bless me.

CREON: Say the truth.

POLYNEICES: That is the truth.

OEDIPUS:
And you want to attack Thebes with my blessing?

POLYNEICES: I have seven battalions total.
Enough to do some real damage against Thebes.
But truthfully, not enough.
I know it.

CREON: We all know it.

POLYNEICES: Oedipus!
I come almost broken to you,
For myself and my allies,
We, the Seven against Thebes,
Who have our spears pointed at her gates,
Waiting for my word to charge,
Waiting for my word to die a helpless death with no
  victory.
Help me Father!
Help me!
You are hope to me.
What the Blind Seer told me about you,
You are my hope.

OEDIPUS: What did she say?

POLYNEICES:
That you can restore the rightful house of Oedipus.

OEDIPUS: How?

POLYNEICES: Just come back to Thebes with me.

CREON: Or give him your body.

OEDIPUS: My body, what good is my body?

POLYNEICES: ...

OEDIPUS: Will any one speak?

THE BLIND SEER: *(Offstage)* I will great King Oedipus.
(She wheels herself through the door.)

OEDIPUS: Who is it, Antigone?

ANTIGONE: The Blind Seer of Thebes.

OEDIPUS: What are you doing here?

THE BLIND SEER: I come for your death.

OEDIPUS: I'm dying?

THE BLIND SEER: Were you ever not?

OEDIPUS: Say what you know.

THE BLIND SEER: Or what, you'll torture me?

OEDIPUS: No.

THE BLIND SEER: Oedipus, you gain in death,
What was lost in life.
Your body be blessed,
Lost King of Tossed Thebes.
Grateful be the land under which you lay.

OEDIPUS: My death, this brings me salvation?

THE BLIND SEER: Perhaps.

ANTIGONE: What's the catch?

THE BLIND SEER: He has to decide who gets his corpse.

OEDIPUS: And you rile my family against me.
To dishonor me.

THE BLIND SEER:
Violence set loose, is violence returned, Stupid Man.

OEDIPUS:
I am sorry, Blind Seer, for the pain I caused you.

THE BLIND SEER:
Don't be sorry, my revenge will be penance enough.

OEDIPUS: So Creon, you don't want me to rule Thebes?

CREON: No, you can't even rule your bowels, Brother.
I just want your body.
Eteokles, my king sent me.
And as a loyal subject,
I obey.

OEDIPUS:
And Poyneices, you just want my corpse as a symbol.

POLYNEICES: More like token,
To be exchanged for victory against Eteokles.

OEDIPUS: I feel so stupid, I felt wanted.

CREON: Not wanted,
Just needed.

(Thunder)

OEDIPUS: What's that music?

ANTIGONE: That's thunder.

OEDIPUS: Where's the rain?

THE BLIND SEER: It will come.

OEDIPUS: I am sorry I doubted you Antigone.

ANTIGONE: Don't think on it again, sir.

POLYNEICES: So how about it?

OEDIPUS: How about what?

POLYNEICES: Who will you give your body to?

(Enter THESEUS.*)*

THESEUS: Oedipus, this is Theseus.
I spoke with my council,
You can stay here,
Even die here if you must.

THE BLIND SEER: That was foretold...

THESEUS: What is this a blind convention?

THE BLIND SEER: Oedipus dies in Colonus.

OEDIPUS: It's where I was born.

ANTIGONE: No Father, you were born in Thebes.

THE BLIND SEER: But, what's not foretold,
Is where your body lay,
And who gets to bury you.
Good luck with that.

THESEUS: What's going on?

ANTIGONE: The Blind Seer brought a prophecy,
That my father's body brings glory to his interment
    earth.
The one who buries him will be blessed.

(NEW NURSE *starts wheeling out* THE BLIND SEER.)

THE BLIND SEER: Farewell, Theban.

OEDIPUS: I am sorry for my cruelty, Blind Seer.

THE BLIND SEER: Perchance, after our evensong is sung
    our shades will meet,
Then maybe, we'll be friends, King Oedipus.
(She exits.)

OEDIPUS: King of Athens, this is my family.

(The family says awkward hellos and heys.)

THESEUS: Hello.

CREON:
Once he dies, his body belongs to Thebes, Theseus.

POLYNEICES: No, King Theseus, his body belongs to his
    eldest son, me.

OEDIPUS: Don't I have a say in this?

CREON: Not by law, Oedipus.

THESEUS: Actually being in Colonus,
You are all subject to Athenian law,
And we say, a person can decide his death rites.

CREON: Are you saying that you will deny Thebes its
    rightful claim?
That sounds to me like a declaration of war.

THESEUS: Who are you?

CREON: I am Creon,
And I bring the gilded voice of Thebes.

THESEUS: Oh, it's gilded?

CREON: I will take the body of Oedipus,
As is my right.

THESEUS: That claim befits a young hooligan,
Not a man of your age, sir.
You shame my city,
You shame me,
You shame yourself.

CREON: So be it.

THESEUS:
And you bring the gilded voice of Thebes you say?

CREON: I do.

THESEUS: Then this is the gilded answer of Athens.

(THESEUS *spits at the feet of* CREON.)

CREON: This is your answer to Thebes then, Athens?

THESEUS: It is, Thebes.

CREON: Hey Athens, you would do this for a faithless
    Father killer,
An incestuous reject, the lowest of all men?

THESEUS: This and more for any man that asks for help.
You can go now.

CREON: I will see you next on the field of war.

THESEUS: I doubt it old man,
When was the last time you held a weapon?
We're done here.

CREON: Oedipus, you have always fought against the most direct path.
It will be,
Why resist it?

THESEUS: Okay, good-bye.

(CREON *exits.*)

POLYNEICES: Thank you, fair and noble Theseus.

THESEUS: For what?

POLYNEICES: For granting me justice.

THESEUS: I did no such thing.

POLYNEICES: You executed law, and shunned Creon.

THESEUS: I know,
I was here.

POLYNEICES: For my benefit.

THESEUS: Hmmm.
Oedipus, do you want to go with your son?

OEDIPUS: I love him,
But I don't.
I want to give Athens my body and blessing,
Theseus you are the first man to show me kindness in
    ten years.
For your sake, I want to be buried in Colonus,
Where I was born.

ANTIGONE: You were born in Thebes, dad.

THESEUS: You heard the man, son.
He's an Athenian citizen now.

POLYNEICES: Then Father, you beckon death for me.

OEDIPUS: No son, you call it for yourself.

POLYNEICES: Farewell sir.

ANTIGONE: Brother, listen, please.

POLYNEICES: What?

ANTIGONE: Don't ruin yourself along with Thebes,
Call off The Seven

POLYNEICES: I can't.
We want honor.

ANTIGONE: You want blood, for blood's sake.
Honor is nowhere to be found in such a mess.
You and Eteokles will both die.

POLYNEICES: It's the choice of Eteokles,
He could give me the Theban Throne.

ANTIGONE: Just walk away from it.

POLYNEICES: Walk away…as I do now.
Look upon me, Antigone
You shall not see this face filled with life again.

ANTIGONE: You will lose,
We all will lose.

POLYNEICES: Don't cry for me Antigone.
I am gone.
(Exits)

THESEUS: What's his problem?

ISMENE: He's just lost.

ANTIGONE: And a ghost.

OEDIPUS: Thank you Theseus,
For letting me be buried here.

THESEUS: Why does everyone in your family jump to
   conclusions?

OEDIPUS: What?

THESEUS: You can die here,
But I might not be able to take your body,
I will need to leave it up to my council.

ISMENE: But you said…

THESEUS: No, those guys were just being jerks.
It was fastest way to get rid of them.
So your father can die in peace.
Which I think we all deserve.
No matter, how evil-swollen our life,
We all deserve rest when our last breath falls.

OEDIPUS: Please.

THESEUS: Athens suffers enough troubles,
Without your infested cadaver polluting our ground.
If were up to me,
I would give your body to Eteokles.
But, it goes to council.
(He exits.)

OEDIPUS: *(Getting closer to death)*
I want to die a man,
Tried failed, hurt healed, lived, loved lost.
Tyrant…fool
But undernames upon me, I'm am a man.
And let me be buried… As all men deserve.

ANTIGONE: I will do what I can.

OEDIPUS: Antigone, thank you, for your company.
Don't let your woman's weapons stain your cheeks.

ANTIGONE: I love you father.

OEDIPUS: …Love you.
Rest, come and staunch these ills.

ANTIGONE: Are you in pain?

ISMENE: Do something.

NEW NURSE: We can't do much, Ismene.

(Thunder)

OEDIPUS: The music again.

ISMENE: It's thunder Father.

OEDIPUS: *(Losing a hold on life a little)*
No more fighting.

NEW NURSE: That's wise sir, no more fighting.

(THESEUS enters.)

ISMENE: What did your council say?

THESEUS: They needed to discuss it in private,
We'll know soon.

(Thunder)

ISMENE: Thunder calls again.

OEDIPUS: Antigone…

ANTIGONE: What is it father?

OEDIPUS: Ismene…
Say good-bye.

ANTIGONE: Good-bye?

OEDIPUS: Yes please, now.

(The CARRIER enters.)

THE CARRIER: Theseus, the council has spoken.

THESEUS: Well…

THE CARRIER:
Athens will accept the gift of dying Oedipus.

THESEUS: Then, take him away.

ANTIGONE: Now?

NEW NURSE: He's not dead yet.

THESEUS: My councilors agreed,
He belongs to Athens now.
Take him.

(The CARRIER carries out the dying OEDIPUS.)

ANTIGONE: Where are you taking him?

THESEUS: I can't tell you,
No one can ever know.

ISMENE: He is our father.

THESEUS: If his body be blessed,
It's currency to attract thieves,
No one will ever know where he is buried.

ANTIGONE: Don't cut us from him in his death.

THESEUS: He asked for this girl.
Go.
You are not welcome here.

ANTIGONE: One more kiss for him.

THESEUS: No.
He is gone.

ANTIGONE: Can't we stay for a little?

THESEUS: No.
You and your twice-bred sister can't stay here,
Pain and misery hang about you like sickly perfume.

(Thunder)

THESEUS:
Go, the sky grows angry.
Move along,
You pollute my eyes,
You pallid girls.

ANTIGONE: Yes sir.

ISMENE: What are we to do?

ANTIGONE: We must return to Thebes.

ISMENE: Why, war is to break out.

ANTIGONE: It is the soil in which we belong sister.

ISMENE: Say you.

ANTIGONE: We must watch our brothers die.

ISMENE: No, why?

ANTIGONE: Why do you fight with me?

ISMENE: I don't, Antigone.
I don't.

(ANTIGONE *and* ISMENE *exit one way,* THESEUS *the other.*
Thunder. The sky brightens.)

NEW NURSE: What now?

NURSE: Intermission.

NEW NURSE: Fantastic.
(*Or any personal word that conveys excitement.*)

(*The* NURSES *casually exit.*)

(*Intermission*)

END OF ACT 3

END OF PART 1

PART 2: HONOR FOUND
ACT 4: PHILOKTETES

*(*NURSES *enter and say something fun, like the following, but not necessarily this.)*

NEW NURSE:
How was your intermission, did you get some food?

NURSE: Whatever they served gives me the runs.

NEW NURSE: Thanks for sharing.

(The NURSES *mop.)*

NURSE: Do you smell that?

NEW NURSE: Yes.

NURSE: It smells like a gas leak?

NEW NURSE: It smells horrible.

(Enter NEOPTOLEMUS *and* ODYSSEUS.*)*

ODYSSEUS: Be careful, Neoptolemus, the air in this
   place is infected.
You can smell the rotting flesh.
Oh, hello.

NEW NURSE: Hey.
Don't mind us, we're just trying to clean up.

*(*NEOPTOLEMUS *vomits.)*

NEW NURSE: Great.

(The NURSES *clean the vomit.)*

NEOPTOLEMUS: This place is hideous Odysseus.

ODYSSEUS: Be strong Neoptolemus, Great Achilles' son
This wretched resting ground is where I left Philoktetes
    a decade ago.
Once a great warrior,
Now, a wasted piece of rotting flesh.
He really let himself go after he mercy-burnt Herakles.

NEOPTOLEMUS:
Why would you damn him to such a place?

ODYSSEUS: He was on our ship that sailed to Troy.
He was bitten by a serpent in the foot before we left.
It seemed a small injury.
But as we sailed the foot began to fester tremendously,
It looked like a pestilent cabbage.
We would have pitied him,
But he whined and cried so miserably.
He became a liability.
His misery made us doubt our mission.
The ship voted,
The majority won,
We abandoned him here,
Under the pretense of gathering supplies.

NEOPTOLEMUS: It seems too cruel, Odysseus.

ODYSSEUS: There was a group consensus,
It wasn't me alone.
Don't let pity for Philoktetes interfere with our mission,
    Neoptolemus.
We must deceive Philoktetes to join us back in Troy.
And he must carry the Golden Bow of Herakles.
The Oracle said Troy will fall
Once we have him and the Golden Bow of Herakles in
    our ranks.

NEOPTOLEMUS: I won't fail you.

ODYSSEUS: Good.
I think he's in there.
See the light.

NEOPTOLEMUS: I see it.

ODYSSEUS: Look in.

(NEOPTOLEMUS *goes to the abandoned incinerator. He pulls
out an apple.*)

NEOPTOLEMUS: No one.

ODYSSEUS: Does it look lived in?

NEOPTOLEMUS: Some cans of food, a tattered bed.
Such smells, like Sickness was born here.

ODYSSEUS: What do you have in your hand?

NEOPTOLEMUS: Nothing, just an apple.
(*He puts the apple back in the incinerator.*)

ODYSSEUS: Is the Golden Bow of Herakles there?

NEOPTOLEMUS: No, just damp sticks for fire.

ODYSSEUS: He must have hidden the Golden Bow.
Such a lost, slothful man to hold the greatest treasure
  of the world.

NEOPTOLEMUS: And I really must deceive Philoktetes,
To get him aboard our ship?

ODYSSEUS:
Oh yes, he would never come on his own accord.

NEOPTOLEMUS: Isn't there some honest way?

ODYSSEUS: Don't be so foolish, boy.
Philoktetes is not the victim you want him to be,
He is not easily liked.
After his days with Herakles,
Bitterness poisoned his soul,
Like the snake venom did his foot.
There is not a Greek more willing to take my life.
You must not have compassion.

None.
Do you understand Neoptolemus?
Neoptolemus!

NEOPTOLEMUS: Yes sir.

ODYSSEUS: This is the only hope left for the Greeks.
Since your father died,
Very few Greeks can hold the Trojans back.

NEOPTOLEMUS: Great Ajax can.

ODYSSEUS: |
Yes, but he fights for his own arrogant challenge,
Not for glory of the Greeks
According to the Oracle,
We need Philoktetes and the Golden Bow.

NEOPTOLEMUS: I know Odysseus.

ODYSSEUS: He must have gone for food,
I am sure he will limp back shortly.
You must be ready.

NEOPTOLEMUS: Ready for what?
To trick a crazy, old, lame man.

ODYSSEUS: Resolve your mind against him.
Hate him, you must.
Think of him as your enemy in this land.
Once in Troy he will be our ally when he sees the glory
he once felt.
But here, hate him.

NEOPTOLEMUS: Alright.

ODYSSEUS: You must deceive him.
When he asks who you are,
Tell him the truth: Achilles' Son.
Then say that your father fell most nobly,
Which he did.

NEOPTOLEMUS: When do I start to lie?

ODYSSEUS: Next, say since Achilles has fallen
The Greek Generals caused resentment that infects
  your blood.
Say they heaped shame upon your great Father.

NEOPTOLEMUS: How?

ODYSSEUS: Say Agamemnon granted Achilles'
  Unchinkable Armor to me.

NEOPTOLEMUS: But they are still deciding whether to
  give the Unchinkable Armor to you or Ajax.

ODYSSEUS: But that is where the lie starts.

NEOPTOLEMUS: Oh.

ODYSSEUS: Then throw taunts and hatreds upon me,
Be liberal in your loathing.
Then say, which is the truth again,
That the Oracle foretold that Herakles' Golden Bow
  would bring down the walls of Troy.
And you would like him to help you,
To fire those Charmed Arrows with the Golden Bow of
  Herakles.
Thus, disgracing me, and winning your Father's
Unchinkable Armor for yourself.

NEOPTOLEMUS:
I don't want my Father's Unchinkable Armor.
It's to go the greatest living soldier, clearly Ajax. Or
  you.

ODYSSEUS: Again, my young friend, this is the deceit
  we must play.
See the difference: Truth and deceit?
Lies, honesty: See?

NEOPTOLEMUS: Odysseus, this can't be noble.
Abusing my father's honor,
To trick some sick cripple.

ODYSSEUS: Yes, Neoptolemus, I am aware that your
   nobility disdains this.
Yes, I know that treachery and lies fit you like itchy
   clothes.
But through this,
We will destroy Troy.
And in that, won't there be honor so great for Greece?
This base action is but one short second, in one long
   day.
And you know the Oracle said that you play your own
   role in the fall of Troy.

(PHILOKTETES *enters on a crutch, looking very sick
and ragged, bringing back supplies from somewhere.*
PHILOKTETES *doesn't notice* NEOPTOLEMUS *and*
ODYSSEUS.)

NEOPTOLEMUS: *(Quiet to* ODYSSEUS)
I will do this.
Guilt, shame and compassion no longer know me.
It will be good to get the once great Philoktetes away
from this place of decay.
Go back to the ship,
And let me play my cold role.

ODYSSEUS: Will you be alright?

NEOPTOLEMUS: Depend on it.

(ODYSSEUS *hurriedly exits. It is clear* PHILOKTETES *smells.*
NEOPTOLEMUS *can barely bear him.)*

PHILOKTETES: *(Noticing* NEOPTOLEMUS)
Who's this?

NURSE: Let him tell you.

PHILOKTETES: What disaster brought you here?

NEOPTOLEMUS: No disaster.
No chance.

PHILOKTETES:
No need to look upon me with such disgust.
Who are you?

NEOPTOLEMUS: …

PHILOKTETES: Am I that appalling?

NURSE: Yes.

PHILOKTETES:
Avert your eyes and speak to me stranger.

NEOPTOLEMUS: I am no stranger.
I am a Greek, like you.

PHILOKTETES: A Greek, well well.
I am Philoktetes…
Now you tell me your name, son.

NEOPTOLEMUS: Neoptolemus.

PHILOKTETES: Son of Great Achilles?

NEOPTOLEMUS: Yes sir.

PHILOKTETES: I love your father.
Let me embrace you, son.

(PHILOKTETES hugs NEOPTOLEMUS, who vomits, but he
keeps it in him mouth, and…)

NEOPTOLEMUS: I swallowed it.

NURSE: Gross.

PHILOKTETES: You okay?

NEOPTOLEMUS: Yes.
Sorry.

PHILOKTETES: Sit down.
Let me get you something for that stomach.

NEOPTOLEMUS: Thank you.

(PHILOKTETES gets a drink.)

PHILOKTETES: What fleet brought you?

NEOPTOLEMUS: No fleet, just me, from Troy.

PHILOKTETES: Troy?
You weren't with us, when we first sailed.

NEOPTOLEMUS: No sir, I was too young,
I joined the fight late.

PHILOKTETES: Has it been that long?

NEOPTOLEMUS: Almost ten years now, sir.

PHILOKTETES: Ten years?

NEOPTOLEMUS: Yes.

PHILOKTETES: Here, drink this.

NEOPTOLEMUS: Thank you.
You were in Troy?

PHILOKTETES: You don't know me?

NEOPTOLEMUS: No sir, I never met you.

PHILOKTETES: Have you heard tales about me?
Philoktetes.

NEOPTOLEMUS: No.

PHILOKTETES: Philok-titties?

NEOPTOLEMUS: No.

PHILOKTETES: Am I forgotten?

NEOPTOLEMUS: Maybe so sir.

PHILOKTETES: How hateful people can be.
To not only abandon your body, but your story.
What good are our lives if they hold no morals for
    others?

NEOPTOLEMUS: Maybe none.

PHILOKTETES:
Well, Achilles' issue, behold the wretched Philoktetes.
Just before we set sail to Troy
My foot was bitten by a serpent.

Aboard the boat my foot's flesh began to pus and flame
   and ooze.
It released a rotten stench, unbearable,
As I know you know.
But trust me son, the pain was worse than any smell
   could be.
We stopped here to gather supplies.
Or so I thought.
While I was dressing my wound on the beach,
I saw our party,
Led by Wily Odysseus rowing back to the main vessel.
They left a few cans of food, nice of them, no?
But no can opener.

NURSE: He won't let us help.

PHILOKTETES: They want to sever my foot.

NURSE: What good is it?

PHILOKTETES: What good are you?

NURSE: None, I guess.

PHILOKTETES: See,
I have nothing that could be called comfort.
I was left to live out an unused life.
Misery keeps my wound fresh,
And the poison always burns.
But I would gladly accept more pain,
If I could make Odysseus suffer.

NEOPTOLEMUS: Really?

PHILOKTETES: Yes, are you so amazed?
Do you think I blaspheme for cursing the ideal
   Odysseus.

NEOPTOLEMUS:
No sir, I have never heard words closer to my own.
It is like I spoke them to you,
Rather than you to me.

PHILOKTETES: How so?

NEOPTOLEMUS:
Odysseus and Agamemnon have wronged me,
And need for revenge burns my soul,
Like the contagion burns your flesh.

PHILOKTETES: You?
How would they misuse the son of Achilles?
How could your father let this happen?

NEOPTOLEMUS: Philoktetes, my father, Achilles, is dead.

PHILOKTETES: Great Achilles has fallen?

NEOPTOLEMUS:
Yes sir, a well guided arrow sank in his soft spot.

PHILOKTETES: Oh no, are there no heroes left?

NEOPTOLEMUS:
Of the noble kind, I would say only Ajax.

PHILOKTETES:
I am sorry about your father, Neoptolemus.
All of life's gains are only fodder for the pain caused
    by their loss.

NEOPTOLEMUS: Yes sir.

PHILOKTETES: But I must mourn for Achilles, son.

NEOPTOLEMUS: No, not now, honorable Greek.
Hear my story, and the ending may bolster your tale.

PHILOKTETES: Me?
Bolster me?

NEOPTOLEMUS: Yes, for I am remembering your legacy.

PHILOKTETES:
Now my woeful joke-life comes back to you.

NEOPTOLEMUS: No sir, are you not the same Philoktetes
    that fought with Herakles.
And my grandsire, Peleus?

PHILOKTETES: Yes.

NEOPTOLEMUS: Those are the stories I heard.
The noble tales of you as a heroic young man.

PHILOKTETES: Those days are long over.

NEOPTOLEMUS: Maybe not, sir.
Back home,
I went to see the Oracles.
When I heard news of my father passing in Troy.

PHILOKTETES: What did the Oracles say?

NEOPTOLEMUS: That through my actions Troy will fall.

PHILOKTETES: That's great.

NEOPTOLEMUS: Yes.
So I quickly joined the Greek legions in Troy.
But when my foot first hit the sand crest,
The dishonor began.

PHILOKTETES: What dishonor?

NEOPTOLEMUS:
I had asked to see the body of my Father.
But hastily, his body had been burned.
No rites granted.
No grave.
Just burnt,
Like rotting meat,
Before I could say my goodbyes.

PHILOKTETES: No?

NEOPTOLEMUS: Yes.
Then I asked for his possessions,
His glorious Unchinkable Armor.
Agamemnon had told me that it was awarded as a
   trophy.

PHILOKTETES: A trophy?

NEOPTOLEMUS: Yes.
As I am not yet a proven warrior,
I agreed,
Such glorious Unchinkable Armor should be given to
    the best surviving Greek soldier.
I think my father would have agreed.

PHILOKTETES: Sure.

NEOPTOLEMUS: So I assumed Ajax the Great received
    my Father's armor.

PHILOKTETES:
Ajax was a close second to your noble father.

NEOPTOLEMUS: Yes, sir, no question.
But no,
Agamemnon gave the Unchinkable Armor to the Wily
    Odysseus.
Who instead of fighting battles,
Would rather debate through them,
To bore his enemy to death.
I figured foul play must be at work,
So I asked Odysseus to be noble and true...

PHILOKTETES: Good luck.

NEOPTOLEMUS: I asked him to grant me the
    Unchinkable Armor.
And honor me, honor my father.

PHILOKTETES: And he refused.

NEOPTOLEMUS:
Yes, in front of the all the Greek chieftains.
They laughed and laughed.
So shamed, I quickly boarded a small vessel
And left that hateful place,
That breeds hateful men.
But my boat,
Being ill'quipped for the long journey,
Only could carry me to where I am now.

Stopping to gather supplies for the remainder of the
  journey home.
And finding you now,
A brother so shamed by the Greek heathens.
Well, this may be my lucky day.

PHILOKTETES: Neoptolemus?

NEOPTOLEMUS: What is it?

PHILOKTETES:
You would not deceive me, would you, man?

NEOPTOLEMUS: No sir.

PHILOKTETES: If you did,
You would bring shame upon the Noble name of your
  father.
You know that, right?

NEOPTOLEMUS: What?

PHILOKTETES:
You would not evoke your father's true name,
Then abuse it, right?
Think of the shame that would bring upon your father.

NEOPTOLEMUS: That shame would be unbearable, sir.

PHILOKTETES: Then Neoptolemus, I trust you.

NEOPTOLEMUS: Yes, well, thank you.
Um, I see there are no supplies for me here, so…

PHILOKTETES: I have a few cans of food you can take.

NEOPTOLEMUS: I can't take what little you have.
Thank you though.
I should go, Philoktetes.

PHILOKTETES: Leave, now?
You have only arrived.
Please stay the night,
The waters will be much calmer come morning.

NEOPTOLEMUS: No, I should go.

PHILOKTETES: Neoptolemus.

NEOPTOLEMUS: What is it?

PHILOKTETES: Nothing, it's nothing.

NEOPTOLEMUS: What?

PHILOKTETES: Could you take me home?

NEOPTOLEMUS: Philoktetes, my bark is small...

PHILOKTETES: I understand.

NEOPTOLEMUS: But it can fit one more.
Please, join me.

PHILOKTETES: I would be a burden.

NEOPTOLEMUS: A burden?
No, a boon.

PHILOKTETES: I have your word of honor,
That you will take me home?

NEOPTOLEMUS: Yes.

PHILOKTETES: Upon your father's name?

NEOPTOLEMUS: What?

PHILOKTETES: Do you swear by the noble name of your
    father that you will take me home?

NEOPTOLEMUS: Hm hm.

PHILOKTETES: What?

NEOPTOLEMUS: Of course I do.

PHILOKTETES: You are the kindest of all men.

NEOPTOLEMUS: Well...

PHILOKTETES:
I will not wail like I did to dishearten the Greeks.
I will wrap my foot very tightly, to kill some of the
    smell.

NURSE: Philoktetes, before you make the journey,
You need to cure your body of its infection.
Your foot can't be saved.

PHILOKTETES: Lose my body not in battle?
The shame that would bring me.
No.

NEW NURSE: You know it's true.

PHILOKTETES: Must I Neoptolemus?

NEOPTOLEMUS: No.
I don't think so.

PHILOKTETES: Thank you.

NURSE: What does he know?

(THE CARRIER *enters.*)

THE CARRIER: Noble son of Noble Achilles.

NEW NURSE: Strange night this is.

NEOPTOLEMUS: Are you a friend?

THE CARRIER: I am friendly enough.
I have news for you.

NEOPTOLEMUS: How did you get here?

THE CARRIER: It doesn't matter.

PHILOKTETES: I know this man.
He was there when Herakles died.
Do not trust him, Neoptolemus.

THE CARRIER: I only speak the truth.
Trust me or don't,
It's your proclivity.

NEOPTOLEMUS: Speak up.

(THE CARRIER *and* NEOPTOLEMUS *talk in private, away from* PHILOKTETES.)

THE CARRIER:
The Greeks manipulate you, son of Great Achilles.

NEOPTOLEMUS: How?

THE CARRIER:
Odysseus, won't allow Philoktetes passage.
Once you convince him to surrender the Golden Bow
of Herakles
Odysseus will doom him once more,
To this infected prison.
This time stripped of his only worldly value,
The Golden Bow of Herakles.

NEOPTOLEMUS: Would Odysseus deceive me?
With the chance to rescue Philoktetes,
Would Odysseus leave him here again?

THE CARRIER: Yes.
I must go, you better follow quickly.
Lest you find fate unkind.
(He exits.)

PHILOKTETES: You look sick again.

NEOPTOLEMUS: I'm okay.

PHILOKTETES: Do you need to vomit again?

NEOPTOLEMUS: No, no.
Let's go.

NURSE: *(Getting ready for foot removal)*
Philoktetes...

*(*NEOPTOLEMUS *sits down.)*

PHILOKTETES: Why do you sit?

NEOPTOLEMUS: The wind doesn't seem right.

PHILOKTETES:
All winds seem right that take us from malady.

NEOPTOLEMUS: Yes. It just doesn't seem right.

PHILOKTETES: Death is not stopped for winds that do
not seem right.

*(*NEOPTOLEMUS *rises.)*

NEOPTOLEMUS: Yes.
Let's go.
Gather what you can carry.

PHILOKTETES: It is not much.

NEOPTOLEMUS: Fine, take what you want.

(PHILOKTETES *gathers jars of herbs.*)

PHILOKTETES:
Here is an herb that eases the swelling of my foot.
And one that induces some sleep when the pain is too
much.

NEOPTOLEMUS: Yes?

PHILOKTETES: And a last,
This one just tastes good.

NEOPTOLEMUS: Is there anything else?
Anything valuable?

PHILOKTETES: Yes, my bow,
The Golden Bow of Herakles.

NEOPTOLEMUS: Yes, bring that.

PHILOKTETES: Of course.

(PHILOKTETES, *get a large knife and removes a panel in the
floor. He pulls out Herakles' Golden Bow from its hiding
place.*)

NEOPTOLEMUS:
Is this the famous Golden Bow of Herakles then?

PHILOKTETES: Yes.

NEOPTOLEMUS: May I hold it?

PHILOKTETES: Yes, my friend,
You can have anything I have.

NEOPTOLEMUS: Thank you.

(PHILOKTETES *hands* NEOPTOLEMUS *the bow, he studies its
wonder.* PHILOKTETES *suffers a sudden bolt of pain.*)

PHILOKTETES: *(In pain)*
Oooo.

NEOPTOLEMUS: What is it?
What.

PHILOKTETES: Nothing.

NEOPTOLEMUS: What?

PHILOKTETES: Nothing.

(PHILOKTETES falls in pain, screaming. The NURSES rush to him, and put him on the operating table.)

NEOPTOLEMUS: He suffers.

NURSE: We noticed.

PHILOKTETES: O Neoptolemus,
I tried being strong
To hide my pain
I can't…
Too much.
Go, go!

NEOPTOLEMUS: What do you mean?

PHILOKTETES: Go on without me.
I don't want you to see me like this.

NURSE: We must amputate the foot.

(The NURSES begin removing his foot.)

PHILOKTETES: No, a little more time, please.

NEOPTOLEMUS: Must it happen?

NURSE: Yes.

PHILOKTETES: Oh if only Odysseus could feel this pain,
Or if Agamemnon could rot like this.

NEOPTOLEMUS: What can I do?

NEW NURSE: Stay out of the way.

PHILOKTETES: No, no, no. Not yet. Please.

(The NURSES *continue to remove his foot.* PHILOKTETES *screams throughout.)*

NEOPTOLEMUS: I want to help.

PHILOKTETES: Don't be scared for me.
Just leave me.
Return some day, please,
To fulfill your promise to me
Upon the noble name of your father.

NEOPTOLEMUS: Give me your hand.
I stay, sir.
Be not afraid.

PHILOKTETES: Watch the Golden Bow of Herakles.
Make sure…
It goes not in…
No deceitful hands…

NEOPTOLEMUS: I am afraid it has already.

PHILOKTETES: What?
Whose hands?

NEOPTOLEMUS: Mine.

PHILOKTETES: Cheer up man.
You are my friend.
Look it's there.

NEOPTOLEMUS: What is?

PHILOKTETES: That bright circle,
In the sky.
Do you see it?

NEOPTOLEMUS: No.

NURSE: He's going under.

PHILOKTETES: It's like magic balls.

NEOPTOLEMUS: Is he dying?

NEW NURSE: No.

PHILOKTETES: Will you keep your hand in mine?

NEOPTOLEMUS: I will.

PHILOKTETES: Never was there a man so noble,
So generous.

(The operation is done. The NURSES *clean the stump and put the foot in a bio-bag.)*

PHILOKTETES: Look at my blood run.
The pain seems worse.

*(*NURSE *cauterizes the stump with an iron.)*

NEOPTOLEMUS: All of life is pain and torment,
When we act against our good will.

PHILOKTETES:
What do you mean, noble son of noble Achilles?

NEOPTOLEMUS: I am not noble.
I am a common villain.

PHILOKTETES: No sir.
You have shown me a kindness that very few have.

NEOPTOLEMUS: No I haven't.
I showed you lies.

PHILOKTETES:
Are you going to leave me here and not take me home?

NEOPTOLEMUS: Leave you, no?
But I wasn't planning on taking you home.

PHILOKTETES: Where to then?

NEOPTOLEMUS: My plan was to take you to Troy.

PHILOKTETES: Troy why?
What is this?
Help me up?

NURSE: No, you rest.

PHILOKTETES: This is a trap.

NURSE: Surprise!

(NURSE *hands* PHILOKTETES *his severed foot in the bag.*)

NEOPTOLEMUS:
I thought you were meant to conquer Troy.
But now I see I am a victim of lies like you.
And only the Golden Bow of Herakles is needed to
conquer Troy.
Not you.

PHILOKTETES:
Return to me the Golden Bow of Herakles.

NEOPTOLEMUS: I can't do that.

PHILOKTETES: Why?

NEOPTOLEMUS:
I am bound by the powers that command me.

PHILOKTETES: What powers?

NEOPTOLEMUS: I can't say.

PHILOKTETES:
Neoptolemus, you are the worst of living creatures.
You fake, evil, pride slug.
How could you let the blood of your Father bless your
    veins.
He would be sick to know your dishonor.
What do you think of that son?
You can't even look at me your shame is so great.
Look at my misery! Look.

NEOPTOLEMUS: I see.

PHILOKTETES: Okay, if you are going, go.

NEOPTOLEMUS: I am sorry.

PHILOKTETES: Sorry is a word in an empty sea.

NEOPTOLEMUS: What should I do?

PHILOKTETES: Go, take the bow, villain.
Strip me of everything.

Take my eyes, boy,
Maybe you can sell them for buttons.

NEOPTOLEMUS: I don't know where my honor lies.

PHILOKTETES: I guess that's your problem.
Selfishness is the greatest disease of humanity.
For no other virus has caused more destruction.
And when hope is so weak a medicine against it,
Why should we use it at all?

(ODYSSEUS *enters.*)

ODYSSEUS: Good work Neoptolemus.

PHILOKTETES: Man, do I hate that voice.

ODYSSEUS: Yes, Philoktetes, it is Odysseus.

PHILOKTETES: Then I lose?
For good?

ODYSSEUS: Yes.

PHILOKTETES: Neoptolemus, please, there is hope.
You can still do what is right.

ODYSSEUS: He is doing what is right.

PHILOKTETES:
May dirty sailors claim your wife, Odysseus.

ODYSSEUS: I know virtue and I know truth,
And I see that they lie in degrees,
Like the sun that shines on a gray winter day,
Still is called sun.
Small truths break under larger ones.
Some truths die on the battlefield,
Like soldiers, to win the greater war of truth.
They served a greater army of greater men, of greater
    ideas.
So good-bye, Philoktetes.
Let's to our ship, Neoptolemus,
And leave him to think about his suffering.

PHILOKTETES: Is this what your father taught you?
Lies and trickery?
Where is your nobility?

NEOPTOLEMUS: …

(ODYSSEUS *and* NEOPTOLEMUS *exit.*)

NURSE: They're gone.

NEW NURSE: Now rest.

PHILOKTETES: I can't

(PHILOKTETES *rises from the bed with great difficulty.*
He buries his foot in the hole that held the Golden Bow of
Herakles.)

(NURSES *sing.*)

[Philoktetes' Song Of Discard]

(PHILOKTETES *holds the knife to his wrist, but decides to*
bury the knife with his foot. He returns to his incinerator
home.)

NEW NURSE: At least he didn't kill himself.

(NEOPTOLEMUS *enters carrying the Golden Bow; he is*
followed closely by ODYSSEUS.)

ODYSSEUS: Where are you going?

NEOPTOLEMUS: To cure myself of my crime.

ODYSSEUS: What crime?

NEOPTOLEMUS: My ignorant obedience to you.

ODYSSEUS: My heart breaks for you young Achilles.
Are you going to return the Golden Bow of Herakles?

NEOPTOLEMUS: Yes.

ODYSSEUS: What good would that do?

NEOPTOLEMUS: Right the wrong I have done, Odysseus.

ODYSSEUS: Right the wrong
You did to this lost, cranky hermit.

But, then in return you would wrong the right
Of the honorable sacking of Troy.
Do you want to mock your father,
And all he fought for?

NEOPTOLEMUS: If honesty is mockery, then I do.

ODYSSEUS: You must know,
I will prevent you from returning the Golden Bow of
    Herakles.

NEOPTOLEMUS: I know that you will try.

ODYSSEUS: And I will succeed,
Under the direct power of Agamemnon.

NEOPTOLEMUS: Why did you deceive me?
When you knew we would leave him here,
Why did you tell me we would free him from his
    prison.

ODYSSEUS: You are young.
You live in a world of immediate reactions.
What's now,
What's next,
But not what is several steps ahead.
When you live longer,
You will see that planning requires the disregard of the
    now.

NEOPTOLEMUS: If you are always disregarding the now,
What good is planning for the future now?

ODYSSEUS: That makes no sense.

NEOPTOLEMUS: Yes it does.

ODYSSEUS: Trust me it doesn't.
Look at it this way,
If you knew I was planning on leaving him here,
Would you have convinced him to give you the Golden
Bow of Herakles?

NEOPTOLEMUS: No.

ODYSSEUS: See.

NEOPTOLEMUS: Why can't we bring Philoktetes back to
   Troy with the Golden Bow of Herakles?

ODYSSEUS: He hates Agamemnon and me so much,
He can't be trusted.
He may try to slaughter us in our sleep.

NEOPTOLEMUS: Can we bring him to his home?

ODYSSEUS: There is no time,
For every minute away from Troy is a Greek life lost.
And do you think he would be welcomed at his
   homeland?
An old, deranged, footless man.
The honor he thinks that waits for him, is an illusion.
He would be an outcast in his own land.
It is far better to leave him here,
With his fantasy of greatness.
But we need the Golden Bow of Herakles,
To make Troy crumble.
Are you not wise enough to see this?

NEOPTOLEMUS: Yes, but isn't it said that compassion
   outweighs wisdom?

ODYSSEUS: Whoever said that, was dumb.

NEOPTOLEMUS:
I feel returning the Golden Bow of Herakles is right.

ODYSSEUS: I know you feel that, but you are wrong.

NEOPTOLEMUS: I know what you think.

(ODYSSEUS *slowly makes a fist.*)

ODYSSEUS: Look at my hand.
It made a fist.

(NEOPTOLEMUS *follows by making his own fist.*)

NEOPTOLEMUS: See you mine,
It did the same.

ODYSSEUS: I see,
And see you my hand unfurl.
Know you my meaning?

NEOPTOLEMUS: I do, Odysseus.
I will fight you.

ODYSSEUS: And you will lose, my young friend.

NEOPTOLEMUS: I know.

ODYSSEUS: I am going to leave you to make whatever
    peace you can with Philoktetes,
But know this,
I will leave this infected place with the Golden Bow of
    Herakles.
The only question is: what side are you on?

(ODYSSEUS *exits.*)

NEOPTOLEMUS: Philoktetes, come out.

(PHILOKTETES *enters.*)

PHILOKTETES:
Have you come to dump more pain upon me?
Do you want my other foot?

NEOPTOLEMUS: No, I come to bring you comfort.

PHILOKTETES: Your comfort is more painful than most
    people's hatred.

NEOPTOLEMUS: I have come back to say I'm sorry.

PHILOKTETES: I can do without your empty words.

NEOPTOLEMUS: Then receive this.

(NEOPTOLEMUS *tries to give the bow to* PHILOKTETES, *who
will not receive it.*)

PHILOKTETES: What are you trying to do?

NEOPTOLEMUS: I am doing what is right.
You can have the Golden Bow of Herakles.
It is yours to defend when Odysseus returns.

PHILOKTETES: I see,
You want to absolve yourself of guilt.

NEOPTOLEMUS: No, I am doing the right thing.

PHILOKTETES: "Right" by your standards,
But the result is the same.
Either way Odysseus is leaving with the Golden Bow
    of Herakles.
The only difference is that in this scenario,
I get beaten up.

NEOPTOLEMUS: Well, I wish you luck.
Let me return this Golden Bow to you.

PHILOKTETES: I see you choose to not make a choice.
Good luck to you then.
Let the tide take you where it wants.
But that does not absolve you of the responsibility of
    choice.
You must do something,
You must choose to do something,
And you must confront your own action.

NEOPTOLEMUS: Take this weapon back.

PHILOKTETES: No.

(NEOPTOLEMUS *forces the Bow on* PHILOKTETES.)

PHILOKTETES: And this seems less cruel to you?

NEOPTOLEMUS: I have no gauge any more.

(ODYSSEUS *enters.*)

ODYSSEUS:
The Golden Bow of Herakles belongs to no man alone,
But to all of Greece now.

PHILOKTETES: Then I shall share it with you.

ODYSSEUS: Thank you Philoktetes.

(PHILOKTETES *loads an arrow to fire at* ODYSSEUS.
NEOPTOLEMUS *pushes* PHILOKTETES *back and blocks the*

arrow with his hand. It gets shot in NEOPTOLEMUS' *hand, and remains there.)*

NEOPTOLEMUS: *(Staring at his hand.)*
Wow, this is not a good day for me.

PHILOKTETES: Is that stuck through your hand?

NEOPTOLEMUS: Yes, yes it is.

(NEOPTOLEMUS *scream in pain. The* NURSES *rush help him.)*

ODYSSEUS: You stupid selfish man.

PHILOKTETES: Me stupid?
Me selfish?

ODYSSEUS: Give me the Golden Bow of Herakles.

NEOPTOLEMUS: Odysseus, help me.

ODYSSEUS: What?

NEOPTOLEMUS: Go to the boat,
Bring me that box I brought.

ODYSSEUS: What's in it?

NEOPTOLEMUS: Just go get it.

ODYSSEUS: Isn't there something here that can help.

NEOPTOLEMUS: Please go.
Hurry.
Get that box.

ODYSSEUS: I'll be back with your box.
(He hastily departs.)

PHILOKTETES: You should have let me kill him.

NEOPTOLEMUS:
Right, that would have settled this matter with honor.

PHILOKTETES: Honor?
Greece knows no honor,
Greek generals are cowards who talk of honor…

NEOPTOLEMUS: They aren't.
They fight with honor, and surety, and dignity.
They are, at times, misguided by their own fantasies.
But who among the living is not.
You have your charmed weapons,
Now is there anything else I can do for you?
Run, limp away, hide, before Odysseus returns. Go!

PHILOKTETES: Does it hurt?

NEOPTOLEMUS: No, feels great.

(NEOPTOLEMUS *tries to pull out the arrow. Everyone panics*)

PHILOKTETES: No don't take it out!
Let the Nurses do it.

NURSE: Thank you.

(*The* NURSES *use saws, shears and some other stuff, trying to break off the arrowhead, nothing seems to work.*)

NEOPTOLEMUS: Why don't you go?

PHILOKTETES: I know your goodness,
As I know my baseness.
You are worthy of your birth.
Worthy to be called your father's son,
Who as a shade wandering the land,
Still shines brighter than most men.

NEOPTOLEMUS: Thanks.

PHILOKTETES: Could you keep your word of honor?

NEOPTOLEMUS: What word of honor?

PHILOKTETES: May I sail with you?

NEOPTOLEMUS: To your homeland?

PHILOKTETES: Yes.

NEOPTOLEMUS: Against knowledge of the impossible,
I will keep my previous word,
And return you to your homeland,

You crazy old man.
How? I don't know yet.

PHILOKTETES: Thank you.

NEOPTOLEMUS: Why don't you come to Troy?

PHILOKTETES: Why would I?

NEOPTOLEMUS: Because the Golden Bow of Herakles is
fated to bring down Troy.
You may as well have the honor of firing the Charmed
Arrows.

PHILOKTETES:
I will not fight for those that dishonored me.
But if you, personally, are in need, then call on me.
And I will give whatever help a one-footed man with a
Golden Bow can give.

NEOPTOLEMUS: When Odysseus returns.
Validate my story,
Temporarily swallow your rage.
And I promise,
Rather than what I say to Odysseus,
I will deliver you home.

PHILOKTETES: More lies?

NEOPTOLEMUS: I do not know what else to do.
One lie spins a web of others.

(*Enter* ODYSSEUS *with a small box.*)

ODYSSEUS: This box?

NEOPTOLEMUS: Yes, thank you.
(*He opens the box, takes out some minties and pops them in
his mouth.*)

ODYSSEUS: You sent me for minties?

NEOPTOLEMUS: Yes, you want some?

ODYSSEUS: No, thank you.

NEOPTOLEMUS: While you were gone,
I took a lesson from your crafty speech,
I was able to convince Philoktetes to join us in Troy.
And he knows his place under you and Agamemnon.
He is yours to command.
As long as he can launch the victorious Charmed
    Arrows over the walls of Troy.

ODYSSEUS: Really?

NEOPTOLEMUS: Yes, tell him what you said to me.

PHILOKTETES: Okay.
Through my hatred of you, Odysseus
I longed for the absent embrace of friendship.
And Neoptolemus, convinced me it would come.
For forgiveness has to start someplace,
And it shall,
In my breast.
Start.
For you.
Yay!

ODYSSEUS: Oh Philoktetes, these words are kinder to
    me than hearing of the fall of Troy.
For I, like you, miss my friend.
And I am sorry I harbored such hatred for you.
I see now that all of the suffering we wish on others,
Is the suffering we wish upon ourselves.
For shame.

PHILOKTETES: That's true.

(ODYSSEUS *embraces* PHILOKTETES *who doesn't hide his
unhappiness.* NEW NURSE *whacks the arrow with a hammer
and the head breaks off.* NEOPTOLEMUS *screams.)*

NEW NURSE: It's out.
It's out.

(NURSES *put a bandage on* NEOPTOLEMUS.)

NEOPTOLEMUS: Thank you.

NEW NURSE: You bet.

NEOPTOLEMUS: Now to the ship,
Where I have enough minties for everyone.

ODYSSEUS: That's probably what made you throw up.
(He exits.)

NEOPTOLEMUS: Do you need help?

PHILOKTETES: Go ahead.
Let me gather some of my belongings.
Thank you.

NEOPTOLEMUS:
I still have no idea how I am going to get you home.
(He exits.)

PHILOKTETES: Oh to say those words to Odysseus,
I would rather my tongue rot.
But in exchange to see my home...

(The SHADE OF HERAKLES *appears.)*

SHADE OF HERAKLES: Hello my Friend.

PHILOKTETES: Herakles, my lord.

SHADE OF HERAKLES:
I am only his shadow, you cannot embrace me.

PHILOKTETES: Why have you come?

SHADE OF HERAKLES: It is good to see you.
I come to turn you from your hatred.

PHILOKTETES: Why?

SHADE OF HERAKLES:
To show that you meant those words to Odysseus.
That the only deception you have is toward yourself.
Move your feet- foot down the path of the right.
Not that of the shallow slothful man.
Listen, I labored for pride lust.
And where did all my pride lust get me.
Where did my dishonesty with Dejanira get me.

What have I accomplished?
Only a funeral pyre, and some stories.
Go to Troy, and help your friends.
And when you are a shade like me,
You will know you lived for honor and love,
For virtues larger than revenge, or spite or laziness.
The only life worth living, is one that leaves people
    better.
You have my gift of my Golden Bow,
Now please pass that gift to others.
Whether they deserve it or not, is not the question.
For if they are corrupt,
Let your kindness crack their corruption,
And leave them better men.

PHILOKTETES: Oh, for how I longed to see your face, my
    friend, not consumed by fire.
I am, as always, at your service,
And will obey your every word.

(*The* SHADE OF DEJANIRA *enters and waits for* HERAKLES.)

SHADE OF HERAKLES: I must go.
Good bye.

(*The* SHADE OF DEJANIRA *and the* SHADE OF HERAKLES
exit back to the underworld.)

PHILOKTETES: I bid you farewell my friends.

(NEOPTOLEMUS *enters.*)

NEOPTOLEMUS: Are you coming?

PHILOKTETES: Can I ask you something?

NEOPTOLEMUS: Sure

PHILOKTETES: Your father's Unchinkable Armor,
Was it really awarded to Odysseus?

NEOPTOLEMUS: Agamemnon and Menelaus are still
    deciding between Odysseus and Ajax.

PHILOKTETES: Then take me to Troy.

NEOPTOLEMUS: Troy?

PHILOKTETES:
I can't let them do to Ajax what they did to me,
For their honor as much as Ajax's.
It's time we stopped treating each other like animals.
Then maybe we can end this decade of death.

NEOPTOLEMUS: Yes sir.

PHILOKTETES: Good-bye my prison.
Good-bye to my hatred and coldness toward living
    men.
Good-bye to the nothingness I have done.
Now, I sail toward humanity, compassion, honor.
Good-bye.

NURSE: Good-bye.

(PHILOKTETES *gives his apple to* NURSE *and limps off with*
NEOPTOLEMUS. NURSES *stand around idle for a second.*)

NEW NURSE: Now what do we do?

NURSE: Let me show you where we keep the drugs?

NEW NURSE: I love drugs.

(*The* NEW NURSE *runs off in excitement, the other* NURSE
follow.)

END OF ACT 4

ACT 5: AJAX

(The empty stage turns into night. There is the sound of sheep bleating. A FLOCK OF SHEEP enter the stage, and run around in the night.)

FLOCK OF SHEEP: Baa.
Baa.
Baa.

(AJAX enters with a giant meat-cleaver, the SHEEP stop bleating and stare at him. AJAX stares at the FLOCK OF SHEEP.)

FLOCK OF SHEEP: Ajax.
Baa.
Ajax.

(The FLOCK OF SHEEP runs around AJAX, he starts getting a terrible head-ache. The bleating becomes loud and chaotic, almost unbearable. Then suddenly, three SHEEP snap into men: AGAMEMNON, ODYSSEUS and MENELAUS, wearing fake sheepskins over military outfits. The rest of the SHEEP still wander around.)

AGAMEMNON: Next order of business,
To honor the Fallen Achilles,
As was his dying wish,
We present his Unchinkable Armor to the next best soldier…

MENELAUS: Drum roll!

AGAMEMNON: Odysseus!

(They bleat like sheep and applaud.)

ODYSSEUS: I don't know what to say.

AJAX: How about something like,
"I don't deserve Achilles' Unchinkable Armor,
Ajax does."

AGAMEMNON: Ajax.

AJAX: Agamemnon,
Sorry to disrupt your little meeting here.
Odysseus, Menelaus.

MENELAUS & ODYSSEUS: Ajax.

AJAX: Why are you guys meeting all the way out here?

MENELAUS: This is where we meeeeeet.

AJAX: I guess I wouldn't understand, right?

MENELAUS: Yes, Ajax, riiight.

AGAMEMNON:
Look Ajax, we don't want any pains from you.
The Unchinkable Armor was awarded to Odysseus by
    a fair vooooote.

AJAX: I didn't come here to debate.

MENELAUS: Then why have you come?

AGAMEMNON: Look at him.

ODYSSEUS: He's craaaaazed.

AGAMEMNON: He's come to butcher uuuuus.

AJAX: If needed, 'twill be done.

ODYSSEUS: Please, go back to your tent.
Go baaaaack to sleep.

AJAX: I will…
When you give me Achilles' Unchinkable Armor.

AGAMEMNON: We gave it to Odysseus, Ajaaaax.

AJAX: Achilles said the armor was to go to the next best
soldier.

AGAMEMNON: And it haaaaaaas.

AJAX: Odysseus is not a better warrior than me.

AGAMEMNON: No Ajax.
But good soldiers aren't waaaaarriors.

MENELAUS: Not any mooooooore.

AJAX: What do you mean?

ODYSSEUS: This war doesn't neeeeeeed warriors.

MENELAUS: It neeeeeeeds politicians.

(AGAMEMNON, MENELAUS *and* ODYSSEUS *start wandering
around aimlessly, doing little sheep things.)*

AGAMEMNON: We tried for ten years to beat the Trojans
with warrior will.

MENELAUS: And to what avaaaaaail?

ODYSSEUS: The bodies keep piling up.

AGAMEMNON: We need strategies, words, ideeeeeeeas.

AJAX: Ideas will beat the Trojans?

AGAMEMNON: Warriors are relics, Ajax.
Museum displays,
Frozen in poses,
But not practical.
Having value only in what we can study from them.

AJAX: I don't like to study.

MENELAUS: No, you certainly don't, maaaaaaaan.

(They all laugh and bleat.)

AJAX: You all shame me,
You shame my work.
You shame my father
Who fought here with Herakles and Philoktetes.
You shame your selves.

AGAMEMNON: Shame ourselves?
The only shame here is what you brought.
Coming here, interrupting these things you don't
   understaaaaaaaand.
We don't need you any more.
You were a good warrior, slaughtering Trojans,
Like some kind of rabid beast,
But the world has moved on.
It's no longer a waaaaar of strength.

AJAX:
Will you give me the Unchinkable Armor of Achilles?

MENELAUS:
Maaaaaan, do you have a brain in that skull cage?
Listen, you will not get the Unchinkable Aaaaaaarmor.

AJAX:
Then Menelaus you will not live to see the sun again.

AGAMEMNON: Excuse me.

(AJAX *attacks the men overcoming them all easily. They
scream and bleat.* AJAX *is covered in their blood.*)

ODYSSEUS:
Ajax, have compassion for us helpless animals.

AJAX: Compassion, when you have none?
I deserve that armor, Odysseus.

(AJAX *sends a death blow to* ODYSSEUS. *Then*
AGAMEMNON, ODYSSEUS *and* MENELAUS *spring up to
their feet and run around bleating like scared animals. The
other* SHEEP *run around scared.*)

AGAMEMNON: Politics, baaa, politics.

ODYSSEUS: Ajax.

AJAX: Odysseus?

MENELAUS:
The aaarmor still belongs to…drum roll, Odysseus.

(AJAX *kills all the men again.* ODYSSEUS, MENELAUS *and* AGAMEMNON *rise again, even more scared this time.*)

AJAX: Again?

(AJAX *kills them again, event more violently, and gets covered with more and more blood.* EURYSAKES *enters, wearing dog ears, and a tail.*)

EURYSAKES: Father Ajax.

(AJAX *is about to swing his giant cleaver at* EURYSAKES, *but stops himself.*)

AJAX: Eurysakes, my son, this is no place for you. Where's your mother?

EURYSAKES: Look at this mess.
This must be buried.

(EURYSAKES *starts digging in the dirt like a doggie.*)

AJAX: You can't bury these shameful men?

EURYSAKES: No, I come to bury you.

AJAX: What?
Am I dead?

EURYSAKES: Not yet.
Woof.

AJAX: What are you doing, son?

EURYSAKES: Woof.

(EURYSAKES *exits on all fours.* ODYSSEUS, MENELAUS *and* AGAMEMNON *rise again and run around like sheep.* AJAX *again slaughters them all savagely. One* SHEEP *is trying to stop* AJAX, *he stabs the sheep. As* AJAX *snaps the neck of his victims, the* SHEEP *he stabbed stands and takes off the sheepskin. It is* TEKMESSA, *covered in blood.*)

TEKMESSA: Ajax!

AJAX: Tekmessa, my wife.

TEKMESSA: You killed them, husband.

AJAX:
They gave Achilles' Unchinkable Armor to Odysseus.
They said the world was politics.
That I was useless.
They shamed me Tekmessa.
They shamed us.
I needed to kill them, my love.
To have honor.

TEKMESSA: Ajax...

AJAX: They deserved it.
Killing is all I know.

TEKMESSA: Ajax.
These aren't men.
You killed animals.

(The bleating slowly starts again.)

AJAX: What?

TEKMESSA: You're in a pasture.

AJAX: What?

TEKMESSA: Ajax, husband, look.

(AGAMEMNON, ODYSSEUS *and* MENELAUS *take of their sheepskins, leave them on the stage and ceremoniously exit, making sheep noise, or laughing; along with all the* SHEEP. *There should be a pile of bloody sheepskins littering the space.)*

TEKMESSA: I'm sorry, Ajax.
You're not well.

AJAX: I'm not?

TEKMESSA: No, you're not.
I was here watching you.
It was...

AJAX: Why didn't you stop me?

TEKMESSA: I tried.
I was invisible to you.
But we need to leave, Ajax.
They will come to kill you.

(The NURSES *enter with some drugs.)*

NURSE: What happened?

TEKMESSA: Ajax planned to murder the Greek Generals,
But in his mad-rage gluttony-blindness of the night,
He thought animals were his victims.

NURSE: We're gone for five minutes...

NEW NURSE: Do you need anything?

TEKMESSA: No, thank you.

(The NURSES *not sure what to do, just go about their normal business.)*

AJAX: I don't want this life any more.

TEKMESSA: We cannot solve horror with horror,
Agony births agony.

AJAX: Animals?

TEKMESSA: You're sick Ajax.
We should go.

AJAX: I can't.
Where would I go?
I can't run from this?

TEKMESSA: What do you want?
It's a new world now, everything is changed,
You changed it without changing yourself.
Let's get our son and go.

AJAX: Can we measure honor by the pound?
By the day?

TEKMESSA: What? What does that mean?

AJAX: Hour on hour, losing honor like weight,
Where's the glory in such a diet?
Where is the honor lost?
Where does it go?
Can you weigh it?
Count it?
Do you gain it back in death?

TEKMESSA: No, Ajax, nothing is gained in death.

(EURYSAKES *enters, very grossed out by the blood.*)

EURYSAKES: Mama.

AJAX: Eurysakes, Son.
I know you are scared.
But children should know while young
The cruel course of the world.

TEKMESSA: Ajax, let's go.
They will come soon,
There is no time.

AJAX: There is never time,
And there never was.
I should kill you, boy,
So you won't have to live in my shadow shame.
But I won't, I can't.
Don't worry.

EURYSAKES: I can revenge this when I am older, sir.

AJAX: The only revenge you should take against this,
Is to live a life of happiness.
Don't let my spoiled life spoil yours.
Alright, Eurysakes, alright.
You will be a good man,
Unlike me.

EURYSAKES: I will be a great soldier to honor you.

AJAX: No, no no.
The world does not want soldiers.

Give the world words and thoughts.
And you will find happiness.
Look how the world treats soldiers. Look.

EURYSAKES: I see.

AJAX: *(Feeling a head pain)*
Why did you bark?

EURYSAKES: I didn't.

AJAX: Don't play now.

EURYSAKES: I'm not.

AJAX: Go. Go.

(AJAX *scares* EURYSAKES *away.)*

TEKMESSA: Why did you scare him away?
We have to leave.

AJAX: We shouldn't cry for what needs to be done.
The doctor does not cry for the tumor he is to trench.

NURSE: He doesn't, it's true.

AJAX: My shame is complete here.
My body is cured of its anemic honor.

TEKMESSA: We adapt or we decay, Ajax.

AJAX: Adapt or decay.
You're right.
I'm a glutton,
I want too much.

TEKMESSA: What does that mean?

AJAX: I am going to the sea.
Where the waves clean the sand,
To wash.

TEKMESSA: Let me come with you.

AJAX: No.

TEKMESSA: You're just going to wash?

AJAX: Yes.

TEKMESSA: And then we leave?

AJAX: I am done with this land, with this war,
After today,
Ajax will not be called a soldier.

(AJAX *embraces* TEKMESSA.)

TEKMESSA: Ajax...

AJAX: What?

(TEKMESSA *collapses the* NURSES *rush to her and hold the wound on her stomach.*)

TEKMESSA: You stabbed me, my love.

AJAX: I'm sorry.

TEKMESSA: Ajax, you didn't know.
You were sick, you were sick.
Ajax, my life, my love
Live to see the sun.

(THE CARRIER *enters.*)

THE CARRIER: I carry a message sir.
First Philoktetes,
Who has just returned from his island prison,
Out of honor to your father,
Comes to your aid.

AJAX: Philkotetes?

THE CARRIER: Yes, and I bring news from the Oracle,
Live to see the sun...

(TEKMESSA *dies.*)

NEW NURSE: She's gone.

AJAX: Prophesies can't help the cleft flesh.

THE CARRIER: That's true.

AJAX:
I don't know where fantasy ends and flesh begins.

THE CARRIER: Does it matter?

AJAX: I guess not.

(THE CARRIER *exits.*)

(NURSES *sing as underscoring:*)

[The Farewell Song To Hero Ajax]

AJAX: Time makes all of us obey.
Winter snow obeys to spring sun.
Dark night obeys to morning's dawn.
This day's life obeys to sleep.
I know when I am beaten,
And I can find peace in that.
(*He kills himself with his meat-cleaver.*)

NURSE: There wasn't much we could do to sort
  through that one.

(EURYSAKES *enters.*)

EURYSAKES: Have you seen my father?

NURSE: Yes.

(NURSE *point to the body of* AJAX.)

EURYSAKES: Oh.

NURSE: He was sick Eurysakes.

EURYSAKES: What do I do now?

NURSE: Mourn.

(*Enter one-footed* PHILOKTETES *and* NEOPTOLMEUS.)

PHILOKTETES: Are you Ajax's boy?
Put your weapon down, we're here to help.

EURYSAKES: Who are you?

PHILOKTETES: I am Philoktetes,
I was a friend to Ajax

NEOPTOLEMUS:
I'm Neoptolemus, Achilles was my father.

EURYSAKES: This is my father.

(EURYSAKES *goes to the body,* PHILOKTETES *stops him.*)

PHILOKTETES: Don't.

EURYSAKES: What?

PHILOKTETES: Don't touch him.
Ajax is a criminal for plotting murder.

NEOPTOLEMUS: Touching him will be a crime.
They'll expect him to rot out here.

EURYSAKES: I just want to help.

PHILOKTETES: Help by finding your way home son.
Can you do that?

EURYSAKES: Like home home?

PHILOKTETES: Yes.

EURYSAKES: I think so.

PHILOKTETES (*to* NEOPTOLEMUS)
Take him to safety.

EURYSAKES: But what about my father.

NEOPTOLEMUS: Philoktetes will take care of this.
Come on.

PHILOKTETES: I'm sorry son.

(EURYSAKES *exits with* NEOPTOLEMUS.)

PHILOKTETES: Ajax, what good will come of this?
Hold still.
This will not hurt you.

(PHILOKTETES *pulls the cleaver from* AJAX's *body. Enter*
ODYSSEUS *carrying Achilles' Unchinkable Armor.*)

ODYSSEUS:
You know, by touching that body, you will be killed.

PHILOKTETES: That sounds like a threat, Odysseus,
Will you enforce it?

ODYSSEUS: No, not me friend, but Agamemnon.
Ajax is criminal,
Trying to bury him is a crime.

PHILOKTETES: What else should I do?

ODYSSEUS: Don't get involved, Philoktetes.
We only just returned,
Don't you want Agamemnon's favor.

PHILOKTETES: I do, Odysseus, but I can't just let this go.
I owe his father something.

ODYSSEUS:
But, know, you will only bring trouble,
By trying to bury Ajax.

PHILOKTETES: What do you think I should do?
Leave him here to let the crows claim his body.

ODYSSEUS: I don't know,
I don't.
I should go,
Agamemnon is coming.
He won't be happy,
And I really can't be involved.

PHILOKTETES: Congratulations, by the way.

ODYSSEUS: On what?

PHILOKTETES:
Being awarded Achilles' Unchinkable Armor.

ODYSSEUS: Let him be Philoktetes.
Let him be.

(*Exit* ODYSSEUS. AGAMEMNON *enters carrying a scepter
and eating an apple. He is followed by* MENELAUS.
PHILOKTETES *holds the Golden Bow as a weapon.*)

AGAMEMNON:
Philoktetes, I didn't expect to see you here.

PHILOKTETES: Agamemnon. Menelaus.

MENELAUS: Mister Philok-titties

AGAMEMNON: Is that the Golden Bow of Herakles?

PHILOKTETES: It is son.

MENELAUS: Sure is nice.

AGAMEMNON: Lower it,
We're not here to fight you.

PHILOKTETES: Then why have you brothers come?

AGAMEMNON:
We came to see who wanted to bury Ajax.

MENELAUS: And look, it's Mister Philok-titties.

PHILOKTETES: I will bury him, Agamemnon.
As demands the honor I owe to him.

AGAMEMNON: Don't let it go like this Philoktetes.

PHILOKTETES: How should it go?

AGAMEMNON: You are welcome back here.
I am glad you came,
I am glad you brought the Golden Bow of Herakles.

MENELAUS: But this is a different world now.

AGAMEMNON: The honor you lived by is dead,
It's a dusty book that's never read.
We see the big-picture honor now.
These small acts of so-called justice
Don't add up anymore.

MENELAUS: It's like old math.

PHILOKTETES: I don't think honor is an opinion boys.

AGAMEMNON: Then tell me this:
Where will this end?
What will all your honor add up to?

PHILOKTETES: I will restore Ajax as one of the greatest
Greek soldiers.

MENELAUS: No you won't.

AGAMEMNON: You can't, my friend.

PHILOKTETES: Don't call me your friend just yet, son.
We still have some years between then and now to
  reconcile.

AGAMEMNON: I agree,
But it's hard to reconcile between the points of
  weapons.
We will not fight you.

PHILOKTETES: What do you expect me to do?

AGAMEMNON: Grieve,
Then allow your hatred to pass.
Realize that all this passion is to justify a murderer.

PHILOKTETES:
The murderer lies dead but the killed still walks.

AGAMEMNON: Ajax is my enemy.
Not always,
But now he is.

PHILOKTETES: Agamemnon, why did you give
  Odysseus Achilles' Unchinkable Armor.

MENELAUS: There was a vote, man.

PHILOKTETES: But why this outcome.
Ajax was a better fighter.

AGAMEMNON: It's a new world.
We don't need mindless men marching off to the
  slaughter glen,
We need intelligence,
We need to see the length of this war,
And plan for its end.
This blind march toward small victories,
Isn't helping any one.
Ajax will not be buried,
Although, once, I did honor him.

PHILOKTETES:
There was never any honor in your family.
Pelops, your grandfather,
Was a dumb heathen.
And your father Atreus
Served his brother's son to him as meat.
Your lot is cursed and base.
Isn't it fated, Agamemnon, that your son Orestes will
   be tormented by the Fury Makers.
And who knows what will become of your daughter,
   Elektra?

AGAMEMNON: Do not taunt me with vague threats to
   my family, Philoktetes.

(PHILOKTETES *starts pushing* AGAMEMNON *around a
little, and poking him with the Bow.* AGAMEMNON *resists
fighting him.*)

PHILOKTETES: Your family has never known honor,
And still you hope to curse this man by screaming half-
   truths with a full voice.
Now fight me.

AGAMEMNON: The fact is you are waging a war, for
   which you are the only soldier,
Against the largest army ever assembled, old man.

PHILOKTETES:
And still I will not suffer a fate worse than Ajax.

(PHILOKTETES *sort of attacks* AGAMEMNON, *who quickly
defeats him and takes the Golden Bow.* MENELAUS
watches in shock. AGAMEMNON *steps on the stump of*
PHILOKTETES, *who, understandably screams in pain. Enter*
ODYSSEUS *wearing the Unchinkable Armor of Achilles, it
looks kind of strange on him.*)

ODYSSEUS: Peace, peace.
Agamemnon please, relax.
Can I say something and still have your respect?

AGAMEMNON:
I would be a fool to not listen to you, Odysseus.

ODYSSEUS: You must pardon Ajax.

AGAMEMNON, MENELAUS & PHILOKTETES:
What?

ODYSSEUS: Let Ajax be buried.

MENELAUS: No way.

AGAMEMNON: Odysseus, why?

ODYSSEUS: Do not let your hatred hamper your honor,
   Agamemnon.
Last night, after Philoktetes and I returned,
It all felt weird to me, coming back.
Even though I learned I won this Unchinkable Armor,
It felt like I lost something.
So I started walking, in the night.
Soon, the gentle sounds of the evening gave way to
   distant sounds of suffering sickness,
Primitive terror.
I saw Ajax working in this sopping pasture.
Some demon,
Some titan-like tormentor.
He scared me.
But as I watched him talk with those animals-
Blind, bemused,
And as I watched him slaughter those animals,
Mad, confused,
I saw his face,
Under the blood spray.
And I knew,
Ajax felt the same feelings I did,
Fear. Sadness. Loss.

AGAMEMNON: You feel loss?

ODYSSEUS: I do.
Agamemnon, Menelaus, we aren't the men we were,

Ajax knew that, Philoktetes knows that.
They live for the values we used to.
I don't know why we stopped living like that.
The world is hard,
And the strong men rise above the difficulties,
And how can one maintain honor,
Needing to be so selfish, greedy, gluttonous, just to
  survive.
But Ajax did.
He rose in life and maintained honor.
And he wanted to show us honor,
Push honor back into our hearts.

MENELAUS: By murdering us?

ODYSSEUS: I'm not saying it was a good plan,
But we shamed him.

AGAMEMNON: How?

ODYSSEUS: This armor, I should not be wearing it.
It looks ridiculous on me.
I accept it because it is the will of my superiors,
But as far as fighters go, Ajax was so close to Achilles'
  skill.
And we left him behind.
And we wanted to leave him behind.
Let's not make the same mistake again.
Disgrace Ajax and leave us with nothing of which to
  be proud.

AGAMEMNON: Should I forget an enemy so easily?

PHILOKTETES: Should all of us be judged by a moment
  with in our lives, or by its summary?

ODYSSEUS:
Our enemy so briefly, but so long our friend.
I may meet the same fate one day.
And so may you.
So may your family.

Elektra, Orestes, they are safe now,
But as we see, no one is immune from the sickness of
   time.

MENELAUS:
Each man satisfies his own selfish needs, is that it?

PHILOKTETES:
No, each man acts for other men, and in doing so,
He gets protection from others.

AGAMEMNON: I have so much hatred for him though.

ODYSSEUS: Our hatred is only a dressing over the
   wound of our guilt.
We must rip clean the dressing and expose our guilt-
   wound to the harshness of the elements.

PHILOKTETES: Only then will it heal.

ODYSSEUS: The dressing only makes it fester.

AGAMEMNON: *(Laughing, a little)*
That's funny, some how.
I find that funny,
Do you Philoktetes?

PHILOKTETES: Like ironic, or humorous?

AGAMEMNON: I don't know, just funny.
Don't you think?

PHILOKTETES: No, I mean, I don't get it.

AGAMEMNON: Neither do I.

MENELAUS: *(Really not understanding)*
It's funny to me too, Agamemnon.

PHILOKTETES: Okay.

AGAMEMNON:
Menelaus, could you wait for me back at the camp.

MENELAUS: For what?

AGAMEMNON: I'll be right there.

MENELAUS: Sure.
See you guys later.
(*He exits.*)

AGAMEMNON: He gets kind of needy.

PHILOKTETES: I see that, yeah.

AGAMEMNON: Bury Ajax.

ODYSSEUS: Really?

AGAMEMNON: It is right. I see that now.

PHILOKTETES: Thank you.

(AGAMEMNON *shakes hands with* PHILOKTETES.)

AGAMEMNON: Here's your bow.

PHILOKTETES: It's not my bow, it's all of Greece's now.
You fire the arrows at Troy.

AGAMEMNON: Really?

PHILOKTETES: Yes.

AGAMEMNON: Hey, come by the camp later,
Let's roast up some of Ajax' slaughter.
There'll be enough lamb chops for the whole camp.

PHILOKTETES: Maybe I will, Agamemnon, maybe I will.

AGAMEMNON: You won't, don't you lie to me.

PHILOKTETES: Thanks though.

(EURYSAKES *sheepishly enters with* NEOPTOLEMUS.)

EURYSAKES: I didn't know how to get home.

NEOPTOLEMUS: Sorry, I thought he should be here.

PHILOKTETES:
Come on Eurysakes, let's go honor your sire.

(DEAD AJAX *and* DEAD TEKMESSA *rise and look at*
EURYSAKES *and the rest of the living.*)

AGAMEMNON: I do hope my life ends better,
But I know it may not.

ODYSSEUS: Philoktetes, as much as this man hated me,
I will be his friend today,
And help give him the most honorable burial.

PHILOKTETES:
Thanks Odysseus, for your worthy words,
But I don't think he would want you to bury him.

(DEAD AJAX *and* DEAD TEKMESSA *exit to the underworld.*)

ODYSSEUS: I hoped to help.

PHILOKTETES: You did, you helped.
Eurysakes.

(EURYSAKES *and* PHILOKTETES *exit after* AJAX.*)

AGAMEMNON: Odysseus.

ODYSSEUS: Yes?

AGAMEMNON:
Want to go fire some charmed arrows at Troy?

ODYSSEUS: Yes sir. Very much.

(AGAMEMNON, NEOPTOLEMUS, *and* ODYSSEUS *exit the opposite way.*)

NEW NURSE: Now what do we do?

NURSE: Second Intermission.

NEW NURSE: Awesome. {Or any other personal word
that conveys personal excitement.}

(*The* NURSES *casually exit.*)

(*Intermission*)

END OF ACT 5

END OF PART 2

PART 3: HONOR ABANDONED
ACT 6: ELEKTRA

(Nurses enter and again say something fun, like the following, but not necessarily this.)

New Nurse: How was this intermission for you?

Nurse: Good.

(The lights go out, it sounds like a fuse getting blown. The Nurses walk around with flashlights, looking for a fuse box.)

New Nurse: Was that supposed to happen?

Nurse: Look for the fuse box.

New Nurse: Do you know where it is?

Nurse: Shh.

(Coughing is heard in the darkness, the Nurses light the action with flashlights. There is Orestes, coughing, and the Shade Of Agamemnon.)

Shade Of Agamemnon:
Are you the son of Agamemnon?

Orestes: Yes.

Shade Of Agamemnon: Orestes,
Behold with thy earthly eyes that which they long
  desire.
Yon, is the grave of your noble father.
This is your home.

From which you fled as a gamin at the urging of your
  sister Elektra,
On the very night of your father's murder at the hands
  of your wicked mother.
Do you remember?

ORESTES: Yes.

SHADE OF AGAMEMNON: He returned from Troy.
And the bath he took that evening,
To wash the decade of blood from his skin,
Became his own blood.
He laid pummeled and pierced
Sixty times,
With a scepter,
In the waters.
Do you remember?

ORESTES: Yes

SHADE OF AGAMEMNON:
Orestes, you must think fast and sharp
Be like the scepter-weapon that entered your father's
  heart.
Know your plan.
The sun has set.
Decide your action before any from the house sees you.

ORESTES: *(Coughing)*
Shade, this is my plan.
I will avenge my father's murder, without armies.
I will watch my mother and her lover suffer.
I will be satisfied.
Does that suit you Father?

SHADE OF AGAMEMNON: You remember me?

ORESTES: I do.

(ELEKTRA *screams from offstage.)*

SHADE OF AGAMEMNON: Hark son.
I hear the sound of woman-cries.

ORESTES: I think it is my sister Elektra.

SHADE OF AGAMEMNON: Elektra, my child.

ORESTES: She comes.
We must leave,
We haven't time.

(*Exit* SHADE OF AGAMEMNON *and* ORESTES. *The* NURSES
find the fuse box. The lights snap on to reveal ELEKTRA. *She
is a mess. She lays down lots of apples, then covers herself
with mud, in some sort of ritual.* ELEKTRA *coughs a lot.*
NURSES *sing:)*

[Song Of Elektra's Fever]

(CHRYSOTHEMIS *enters, carrying a box. She is dressed like a
pretty-pretty princess.)*

CHRYSOTHEMIS: Elektra, sister.

ELEKTRA: Chrysothemis.

CHRYSOTHEMIS: How are you feeling?

ELEKTRA: Fine.

CHRYSOTHEMIS: Has your fever broke?

NURSE: It hasn't.

NEW NURSE: She doesn't want to get better.

CHRYSOTHEMIS: You know, rubbing yourself with mud
   will just make you sicker.

ELEKTRA: If you want to help me,
Help me by driving a knife into Wicked Mother's
   breast.

CHRYSOTHEMIS: I can't do that.

ELEKTRA:
Help me by burning Father's throne with Aegisthus,
His cousin and replacement,
Sitting upon it.

CHRYSOTHEMIS: Can't do that either.
Elektra, go home, you should be in bed.
You're sick.

ELEKTRA: What makes me sick is thoughts of them
  sharing the womb in which father planted our seed.

CHRYSOTHEMIS: Well don't think about it.
Gross.

ELEKTRA: Has that fool Aegisthus returned?

CHRYSOTHEMIS:
No, he is set to come back before morning.

ELEKTRA:
I hope Orestes comes back before Aegisthus does.

CHRYSOTHEMIS: It's been over ten years, sister,
Orestes is not coming back.
He is not going to help you.

ELEKTRA: He is.
When I drove him from the bloody scene, he promised.

CHRYSOTHEMIS: But he was a boy.

ELEKTRA: Yes.

CHRYSOTHEMIS:
Like a boy, he didn't believe what he was saying.

ELEKTRA: But he's a man now.

CHRYSOTHEMIS: If he survived.

ELEKTRA: If he is Agamemnon's son, he survived.

CHRYSOTHEMIS: Maybe he did survive,
And maybe he lives free of the horror that feeds your
  fever.

ELEKTRA: No, if we are of one blood,
Our Father, Agamemnon's blood,
Then he is as burning as I.

CHRYSOTHEMIS: It's my blood too,
And I am not as upset as you.

ELEKTRA: Well, you're...different, Chrysothemis.

CHRYSOTHEMIS:
You know, I think what mother did was terrible.
And if I were stronger,
I would show them this friendship that I have for them
    is really hatred,
In, like, a disguise.
But I am too weak to fight against our trouble.
It is best, when beaten,
To give in and obey the victors.
Then at least you appear to be simpatico with them,
And you can benefit from the glories that accompany
    such alliances.

ELEKTRA: Glories, such as dresses, and parties.

CHRYSOTHEMIS: Such as respect and trust and freedom.
But dresses and parties too.

ELEKTRA: You don't act like you hate them.

CHRYSOTHEMIS: But I do hate them.
Life's just easier this way.

ELEKTRA: If you hate them,
Help me plot their murder.

CHRYSOTHEMIS: No.

ELEKTRA: Chrysothemis, I can't do it alone.

CHRYSOTHEMIS: Then don't do it at all.
If we murder them,
Someone will murder us,
Then someone will murder them.
Where would it end?

ELEKTRA: You are your mother's daughter.

CHRYSOTHEMIS:
Elektra and her single-minded obsession.

As you plot a million different ways to destroy our
mother's life,
You are only destroying your own.

ELEKTRA: Tell me I am not justified and I will stop.
I will share your dresses, I will attend your parties.
Tell me this sister,
I have no cause for revenge. Say it.

CHRYSOTHEMIS: You have cause Elektra.

ELEKTRA: See.

CHRYSOTHEMIS: But there is a line that stands between
   what is Just with a big J,
And what is Unhealthy, with a big "You".

ELEKTRA: I stand on the side of the right.
Help me,
Help me end my misery.

CHRYSOTHEMIS: I'm not killing anyone.

ELEKTRA: Coward.

CHRYSOTHEMIS: But a happy well-provided for coward.

ELEKTRA: Your happiness sickens me.

CHRYSOTHEMIS: I will tell you one thing sister.
They are planning on giving you an ultimatum.

ELEKTRA: What?

CHRYSOTHEMIS: It's like a choice.

ELEKTRA:
I know what an ultimatum is, what is the ultimatum.

CHRYSOTHEMIS: Either stop these lamentations, or
   they'll send you away?

ELEKTRA: To where?

CHRYSOTHEMIS: The Cloister of the Sisterhood of the
   Setting Sun, where no visitors come.
So, be wise sister, and stop.

Or perform these rites in your heart.
But have your face look like mine.

(CHRYSOTHEMIS *shows* ELEKTRA *her happy face.*)

ELEKTRA: Flattery is your way,
Not mine.

CHRYSOTHEMIS:
So it is better to fall a disgraced young woman,
Than to suffer a few moments of flattery.

ELEKTRA: If I fall, there will be no disgrace.
I will do so in honor of our Father.

CHRYSOTHEMIS: Father loved you, did he not?

ELEKTRA: Yes.

CHRYSOTHEMIS:
Then why would he want you to suffer?

ELEKTRA:
Honor was more important to him than happiness.
That is why he killed Iphigenia to set sail to Troy.

CHRYSOTHEMIS: Maybe Father's honor system was a
  little perverted, Elektra.

ELEKTRA: You are a fool!
Go back and play with your friends,
I will wait for Orestes to return.

CHRYSOTHEMIS: He is not coming back!
What joy waits for him here?
Just your mud and dirty apples.

ELEKTRA: Something greater than joy.

CHRYSOTHEMIS: It's no point Elektra, I'm going.

ELEKTRA: And where to?

CHRYSOTHEMIS:
Mother sent me to give Father's grave some offerings.

ELEKTRA: What offering?

CHRYSOTHEMIS: I don't know.
(She takes from the box AGAMEMNON's *scepter.)*
Uh-oh.

ELEKTRA: She puts him in the grave yet gives it homage
with the scepter she killed him with?

CHRYSOTHEMIS: Mother believes her act was justified.

ELEKTRA: I know she does.

CHRYSOTHEMIS: Daddy Agamemnon killed our sister,
our young Iphigenia,
Still in her swaddling clothes.

ELEKTRA: As he was ordered to do by the Oracles.
Do not put that on father's grave.
You intend to beat father one more time with the
weapon.

CHRYSOTHEMIS: I am just doing as I am told.

NURSE: Chrysothemis, through her fever, Elektra
talks some sense on this point.

CHRYSOTHEMIS: Then should I give it back to Mother?

ELEKTRA: Give it to me.

CHRYSOTHEMIS:
Alright, don't let Mother know I gave it to you.
If she finds out,
Things will not go well for either of us.

*(*CHRYSOTHEMIS *exits.* CLYTEMNESTRA *enters.)*

CLYTEMNESTRA: Give me that.

ELEKTRA: No, mother.

CLYTEMNESTRA:
I told her to put in on your father's grave.
That girl is so simple sometimes.

ELEKTRA: Like mother like daughter.

CLYTEMNESTRA: You are my daughter too.

ELEKTRA: Don't remind me Wicked Mother.

CLYTEMNESTRA: How are you feeling?

ELEKTRA: Terrible.

CLYTEMNESTRA: Come home,
Let's give you a bath.

ELEKTRA: A bath like you gave Father?

CLYTEMNESTRA: Come home.

ELEKTRA: When I'm done.

CLYTEMNESTRA:
Elektra, it seems that when Aegisthus is home,
He can keep you from haunting this ghoulish place.
But you never listen to me.
This will kill you, Elektra.
Look at you. You are a mess.

ELEKTRA: *(Coughing)*
The outward reflects the inward.

CLYTEMNESTRA: Your father is gone, dear.
Agamemnon is dead, dear.
I killed him, yes.
But am I his murderer?

ELEKTRA: Yes.

CLYTEMNESTRA:
No. I was his executioner, he was the murderer.
He took Iphigenia from my arms, threw her across the
   rock,
And pushed that knife into her plum sized heart.
Why would you value such a baby-killer?
What if it were you he killed?

ELEKTRA: I would have died with honor.

CLYTEMNESTRA: Right, because father knows best.
Come here.

ELEKTRA: Why?

CLYTEMNESTRA: I am going to hug you.

ELEKTRA: I'm covered in mud.

CLYTEMNESTRA: Still, come here.
I'm going to hug you.

ELEKTRA: No.

(CLYTEMNESTRA *does some kind of choo-choo hug dance
for little children, and hugs* ELEKTRA *who resists, but
eventually gives in.*)

CLYTEMNESTRA: Your father killed my precious babe,
And thought not again on the pains of the child,
Or the pain its mother felt.
Then he sailed away to Troy,
To fight a war for the alleged honor of his annoying
     brother, Menelaus
And if you judge me for murder, Elektra,
And harbor hatred in your heart for murderers,
Fester that bile against your sire,
For he is a murderer too.

ELEKTRA: Leave me in peace.

CLYTEMNESTRA: Yes, you will have peace,
When we send you to the Cloister of the Sisterhood of
     the Setting Sun, where no visitors come.

ELEKTRA: You fear me, because you fear your self.

CLYTEMNESTRA: Why do I fear myself?

ELEKTRA: You know you are base and foul and
     murdered a noble man.
And you know you share your bed with the weak
     common fool, Aegisthus,
With father's blood in his veins yes, but diluted by
     awful timidity.

CLYTEMNESTRA:
This decade long pretense against me is ridiculous
It is a show out of some kind of sick perverted jealousy.

An act for some unseen audience.
No one can prolong the fever of hatred this long.
It must end.
It will end.

ELEKTRA: If I am faking sickness, if my hatred toward
  you is pretense.
Then tell me as you lay dying, how real the show
  appears.

CLYTEMNESTRA: Then kill me.
What's stopping you?

ELEKTRA: I don't know, Mama.

CLYTEMNESTRA: Waiting for Orestes, to get him to do
  your bloody work?
He's not coming back, Elektra
He has moved on, this place doesn't exist for him any
  more,
You are a distant dream of his childhood,
He does not suffer from your fever.
He is not going to come here and save you from your
  dejection.

ELEKTRA: Dejection?
This is burning hatred Wicked Mother.
Oh if only Father married a true woman,
Who kept his bed clean,
Instead of a common whore.

CLYTEMNESTRA: Will you apologize for that?

ELEKTRA: No.

CLYTEMNESTRA: Apologize, I am your mother.

ELEKTRA:
Why should I apologize to a dead woman for the truth.

CLYTEMNESTRA: Stay here, girl,
Leave your fruits,
Drown in your mud,

Cough your life out.
Pay homage to a low cheating scoundrel that hid
behind the illusion of nobility,
Make the sufferers suffer more.
When Aegisthus returns tonight, he'll come here and
    drag you home.

(CLYTEMNESTRA *starts to leave, but* ELEKTRA *stops her.*)

ELEKTRA: Mama.

CLYTEMNESTRA: What?

ELEKTRA: Why today?

CLYTEMNESTRA: What?

ELEKTRA: I always come here when Aegisthus is away.
Why today did you meet me here.
Why today did you want Chrysothemis to return the
    staff to Father. Why?

CLYTEMNESTRA: Isn't it time to be over?
I saw the Shade of your father,
Walking among this mud.
This dream... I know not yet it's full meaning,
But the end is to come.
Soon.

(ORESTES *enters, disguised as an officer.*)

ORESTES: *(As an officer)*
Excuse me, could you tell me if I am close to the house
    of Aegisthus.

NURSE: Yes sir, this is it.

ORESTES: *(As an officer)*
And this is his queen, Clytemnestra?

NURSE: Yes sir.

ORESTES: *(As an officer)*
Hail, goodly queen Clytemnestra!
I bring good news for you and your husband.

CLYTEMNESTRA:
I would welcome any good news you have.

ORESTES: *(As an officer)*
He, who plotted your murder, is dead.

CLYTEMNESTRA: Who is dead sir?
I don't know anyone who plots my murder, other than
   this girl here.

ORESTES: *(As an officer)*
Orestes, your son, ma'am.
Orestes is dead.

ELEKTRA: Oh no, no.

CLYTEMNESTRA: How do you know he is dead?

ORESTES: *(As an officer)*
I have here his ashes.
(He holds up an urn.)

ELEKTRA: No.

CLYTEMNESTRA: How did it happen?

ORESTES: *(As an officer)*
He was driving a chariot, with evil intents in his heart.
Afore he left my city, he confessed to planning your
   death.
Upon the road,
The horses reared,
As if conscience bade,
Off the rocky climb into the roughly sea.
There the foam consumed his body.
Until, it appeared on a beach three hours past.
The tide set and there sat Orestes' chariot,
Horses and driver set in proper place but time-frozen
lost.
The sight, 'twas said, to be chilling.
We had his body burnt as is our rite.
And I come to return the ashes to his home land.

Although, I can't assume you will welcome he that
  planned your death.

CLYTEMNESTRA: He was my son, and shall have every
  honor fit for such a relation.
Though he planned my death,
He shall bring no harm to me now.
Oh, I am a mother that grieves for her son.

ELEKTRA: A mother grieving for her son?
And you claim my mourning was false, Wicked
  Mother.

CLYTEMNESTRA: Come inside sir,
We will discuss further proof of those being the ashes
of my son.
Let us away from this girl,
Who offers no threat, but nuisance.

ORESTES: *(As an officer, coughing)*
I do have more proof Madame.

CLYTEMNESTRA: Come inside.

ELEKTRA:
Woe breeds woeful children in this woeful land,
Wicked Matron of the Damned.
How can justice let you live and bleed my noble
  brother?

CLYTEMNESTRA: I told you,
Justice is on my side, you crazy girl.

ORESTES: *(As an officer)*
Are you alright girl?
My heart goes out to you.

ELEKTRA: Keep your heart for yourself.

CLYTEMNESTRA: Come sir, and leave her to wail for her
  imaginary friends of justice.

(CLYTEMNESTRA *and* ORESTES *exit.)*

ELEKTRA: Is there no idol of misery?

NURSE: We don't know.

ELEKTRA:
No idol of cruel torment for me now to worship?
I will lie at the feet of that idol, because that is all I
  know.
I shall become his bride and ride into the atmosphere
  on a chariot of mercury,
Dripping acid over this infected land.
Orestes was my only hope,
Now hope is cut from my body like a hewn limb.
I live. I live pain.
I am pain.
I want life no more.

(CHRYSOTHEMIS *enters.*)

CHRYSOTHEMIS: Sister, I come with happy news!

ELEKTRA: Orestes is dead!
Our safety lost!
Orestes is dead!

CHRYSOTHEMIS: No.

ELEKTRA: I know, it is too much!

CHRYSOTHEMIS: No.
I don't mean, "No, it can't be"
I mean, "No, he isn't dead."

ELEKTRA: What?

CHRYSOTHEMIS: He's back.

ELEKTRA: You mock my pain, like our Wicked Mother.

CHRYSOTHEMIS: No, I tell you, he's back.
It's his childhood toy.
Bear-istophanes

(CHRYSOTHEMIS *shows* ELEKTRA *the stuffed bear.*)

ELEKTRA: Where did you get this?

CHRYSOTHEMIS: It was left on Father's grave-tomb,
As an offering.

ELEKTRA: Is this a joke?

CHRYSOTHEMIS:
No, for my love of you and our brother,
I think he has returned and walks among us.

ELEKTRA: You are cruel to ridicule me now,
If ever you felt pity for me, feel it now, Chrysothemis.

CHRYSOTHEMIS:
Why do you want to feel misery so deeply?
Give it up, Orestes is here.

ELEKTRA: I need your help sister.

CHRYSOTHEMIS: What?

ELEKTRA: Can you be a woman?

CHRYSOTHEMIS: Yes, why?
Yes, I think so.
Why?

ELEKTRA: I need your help.
I need your hand.
I need you to fill the role fated for Orestes.

CHRYSOTHEMIS: Orestes is not dead.

ELEKTRA: He is gone, and I need you.

CHRYSOTHEMIS: Need me for what.

ELEKTRA: It's time.

CHRYSOTHEMIS: No Elektra, no.

ELEKTRA: Yes.

CHRYSOTHEMIS: No, Orestes lives I tell you.
And I will play no role in bringing more death to this
    house.

ELEKTRA: My mind is resolved, the murder will happen
    when Aegisthus returns tonight.

Either you help my hand, and they both shall die,
Or you leave me to solitary action and I die.
So choose,
Do I die,
Or do the murderers?

CHRYSOTHEMIS: No one will die.

ELEKTRA: Before the sun rises, this house once again
    will be red with death,
But you hold the orders for who shall die.

CHRYSOTHEMIS: No, I cannot be guilty for no action.

ELEKTRA: Inaction is the greatest crime.
Choose.

CHRYSOTHEMIS: I choose nothing.

ELEKTRA: Then you have chosen my death.
Today you lose the last of your honest kin.
Go.
Even warn Wicked Mother, it doesn't matter.
My death is scratched in my bone.

CHRYSOTHEMIS: Elektra…

ELEKTRA: Go, Helpless Child of the Wicked Mother.
Go to your dresses and your parties,
And dance on my body,
When Aegisthus leaves it in the yard to rot.

CHRYSOTHEMIS:
Sometimes the world is easier when you worry less.
I am sorry you feel I chose your death.
And you know, maybe I did.
Because, sister, death seems to be the only thing that
would give you peace.
So maybe I did.
Go ahead and die,
Like you want.
Just don't die on my stuff.

(CHRYSOTHEMIS *exits.* ELEKTRA *prepares her self for battle as* ORESTES *enters, still dressed as an officer, carrying the funeral urn.*)

ORESTES: *(As an officer)*
Elektra.

ELEKTRA: Do you come here to tease me?

ORESTES: *(As an officer)*
No miss, your mother wanted me to show you the
    proof of your brother's death.
She feared you would not believe it if she showed it.

ELEKTRA: Well what is the proof, annoying man, then
    leave me to my affairs.

(ORESTES *holds up a locket.*)

ORESTES: *(As an officer)*
This locket ma'am.
Its treasure be your image, in younger days.

(ELEKTRA *takes the locket, and shows her own locket hanging around her neck.*)

ELEKTRA: Aye, sir, and I have its twin.
We traded it in happier times,
In case we ever were sent apart.

ORESTES: *(As an officer)*
Well, now you are reunited.

(ORESTES *gives* ELEKTRA *the urn.*)

ELEKTRA: This is a heavy burden stranger.

(ELEKTRA *and* ORESTES *and* ELEKTRA *cough a little.*)

ELEKTRA: Are you sick?

ORESTES: *(As an officer)*
I've had a fever for a while,
But I think it will clear soon.

ELEKTRA: Me too.

ORESTES: *(As an officer)*
I am sorry I bring this news, and the dust of your
  brother.
Who, it seems, you loved greatly.

ELEKTRA: Yes sir, ever so greatly.
And don't be sorry.
I thank you.
I waited years upon years for my brother's return,
Not fully knowing my life's course,
Anticipating, waiting for action.
And now he has returned I know what must be done.
The memories are heavier than this dust.

ORESTES: *(As an officer)*
Elektra, in mourning you look so beautiful.

ELEKTRA: Thank you sir, but I don't think now is an
  appropriate time to flirt with me.

ORESTES: *(As an officer)*
I don't flirt with you.
I offer you compassion.

ELEKTRA: Then you are the first sir.

ORESTES: *(As an officer)*
You are grossly misused.

ELEKTRA: Maybe. I thank you for your pity.
Will you excuse me, while I bury what is left of my
  brother.

ORESTES: *(As an officer)*
Please Elektra, allow me to help,
For my misery rivals yours.

ELEKTRA: Why boy, are you so moved?

ORESTES: *(As an officer)*
Give me the urn, let me help you!

ELEKTRA: Here it is.
Dig a hole in the earth.
And together we will perform the rites.

ORESTES: *(As an officer)*
Thank you for trusting me Elektra.

(ELEKTRA give ORESTES the urn. ORESTES kneels before ELEKTRA.)

ORESTES: *(As an officer)*
No need to mourn that which has not been lost.
(He opens the urn and flowers emerge.)
Gaze upon the image in your locket, yet living.

ELEKTRA: My brother lives?

ORESTES: If the fire that burns my body be called life,
    then Orestes lives.
(He reveals himself.)

ELEKTRA: Is this your voice that caresses my ear?
Is this your body that shines in my eyes?

ORESTES: It is.

(ELEKTRA and ORESTES embrace.)

ELEKTRA: Oh, do I touch you?

ORESTES: Yes, sister, as I do you.
And always will.

ELEKTRA: Yes!

ORESTES: Yes, sister, yes.

ELEKTRA: That outfit is ridiculous?
You looked like you escaped from an asylum.

ORESTES: I had to improvise a little Elektra.
I could only find and this giant coat and plastic thingy.
I'm surprised it fooled Wicked Mother.

ELEKTRA: Oh, how I missed you, Father's son,
I want to scream for joy.

ORESTES: Yes, but let us be quiet.

ELEKTRA: Why?

ORESTES: We want no one to know what is to come.

ELEKTRA: What, will we do this deed tonight?

ORESTES:
Yes Elektra, now comes the evening. Our evening.
The evening for which we wrought our lives.

ELEKTRA: What must I do to sate our wrath?

ORESTES: Nothing, I will do all that needs to be done.

ELEKTRA: Do not steal from me,
That which so soon was given.
I have long waited too,
Let me not merely wait for the body count.

ORESTES: Elektra, we speak of misdeeds and murder.
Be it just or not, it will not be accepted.
My hands shall wear the blood.
Not yours.

ELEKTRA: But can I watch?

ORESTES: Oh yeah.

(ELEKTRA *hands* ORESTES *the scepter.*)

ELEKTRA: Then enter sir, sate our wrath and bring both
death and joy.

(*The* SHADE OF AGAMEMNON *appears.*)

SHADE OF AGAMEMNON: Foolish children!
Have you senses?
Are you feeling joy at murder!

ELEKTRA: What is this brother?

ORESTES: Do you not see?

ELEKTRA: I do, but I cannot believe my eyes.

ORESTES: This is the Shade of the man who gave us life.

SHADE OF AGAMEMNON:
Do you act this role out of boredom?
For gain of thrill?
Do not find joy in the horrible, children.
Matricide is not to be raveled in revels.
You will be murderers, but not merry-makers.
Where is honor in childish joy?
This is revenge for my death,
This is not a Bull Slaughter Festival!
It is surgery.
The doctor doesn't excite for the tumor to be removed.

NURSE: It's true, He doesn't.

SHADE OF AGAMEMNON: I did not haunt these doors
    decade-long to see you delight in more misery.
Be cold.
Do you do this act for me or for yourselves?

ELEKTRA: For you, sir.

ORESTES: Sir, question us no longer.
I have killed my mirth.

SHADE OF AGAMEMNON: Good cold boy.

ELEKTRA: May I embrace you?

SHADE OF AGAMEMNON:
No, daughter, it is not allowed.

ELEKTRA: But I must, Papa.

(ELEKTRA *goes to embrace the* SHADE OF AGAMEMNON.
Thunder scares her away, the SHADE OF AGAMEMNON
exits to the underworld.)

ORESTES: Elektra, he is gone.
Go bring our Wicked Mother here.
And here she shall fall.

(ELEKTRA *exits.* ORESTES *gets ready for what is about to
come by covering himself with mud. The* NURSES *turn their
backs to the scene about to unfold and sing.*)

[Battle Song]

(ELEKTRA *and* CLYTEMNESTRA *enter.*)

ELEKTRA: You will see Mother, my fears will end.

CLYTEMNESTRA: What is it Elektra?

ELEKTRA: Look upon this man.

CLYTEMNESTRA:
Is this the man that brought news of Orestes death?

ELEKTRA: It is mother.

CLYTEMNESTRA: What news have you now, sir?

ORESTES: News of another death, Madame.

CLYTEMNESTRA: Whose death, sir?

ORESTES: Your own death, ma'am.

CLYTEMNESTRA: Oh, be you, then, Orestes.

ORESTES: I am.
Hello Wicked Mother.

CLYTEMNESTRA: Oh please, son no.

ORESTES: It must be.

CLYTEMNESTRA:
May Aegisthus return before your deed is done.

ORESTES: He won't, for my deed is almost done.

CLYTEMNESTRA: Have pity on your mother, Orestes.

ORESTES: No.

(ORESTES *beats* CLYTEMNESTRA *several times with the scepter.*)

CLYTEMNESTRA: My son, my son, what have you done?

(ORESTES *continues to violently beat her.* ELEKTRA *stops him.*)

ELEKTRA: One guilty one is dead.

ORESTES: You shall live in no more fear, beautiful sister.
This wicked widow can no more spot your goodliness.

(ELEKTRA *and* ORESTES *kiss.* AEGISTHUS *enters running,
with the Golden Bow of Herakles.* ORESTES *covers*
CLYTEMNESTRA.)

AEGISTHUS: Elektra.

ELEKTRA: Aegisthus, uncle father, welcome home.

AEGISTHUS:
I heard that Orestes was dead, is this news truth?

ELEKTRA: Ask this man,
He carried the tale.

AEGISTHUS:
Sir, did you report that my nephew Orestes has died?

ORESTES: I did report that sir.

AEGISTHUS: Why do you look familiar, boy?

ORESTES: Because I am familiar, Aegisthus.

AEGISTHUS: Why are you in your skivvies?

ORESTES: I got hot.

AEGISTHUS: Can I see the body for myself?

ELEKTRA: You can.

AEGISTHUS: Where is Clytemnestra?

ORESTES: She is near.

ELEKTRA: And I have found my way into the heart of
your hostess.

AEGISTHUS: What?

ELEKTRA: Nothing.

AEGISTHUS: Man, show me the body.

(ELEKTRA *takes him to the covered body of* CLYTEMNESTRA.)

ELEKTRA: Here is the body.

AEGISTHUS: This is the body of Orestes?

ORESTES: No.

AEGISTHUS: Where is Orestes' body?

ORESTES: This is, sir.

AEGISTHUS: What body boy?

ORESTES: This body.
The one I live within.

AEGISTHUS: Oh.
Then whose body is this?

ELEKTRA: See for yourself.

(AEGISTHUS *reveals the body of* CLYTEMNESTRA.)

AEGISTHUS: Oh.

ORESTES: Are you scared?

AEGISTHUS: Yes,
If what I see is true,
I know the ending.

ELEKTRA:
For all things righteous, let him talk no further.
How can talking save one from death,
Words are breath and soon run dry.
To me, this will be the greatest revenge mankind has
   wrought.

AEGISTHUS: Please spare me, take this.
It was your father's.
It's the Golden Bow of Herakles.
One of the greatest treasures of the world.

(ORESTES *breaks the Golden Bow of Herakles.*)

AEGISTHUS: Okay…
Have at me then, boy,
I know the outcome, but I will still fight.

ORESTES: Thank you sir.

AEGISTHUS: For what boy?

ORESTES:
Prolonging your death, then I will savor it more.
To my father's grave, there I will finish you.

(AEGISTHUS *runs out.*)

ELEKTRA: Brother, you are smiling.

ORESTES: Yes, how can I not take joy in this, sister.

(ORESTES *exits following* AEGISTHUS. DEAD
CLYTEMNESTRA *rises and walks to the exit.*)

ELEKTRA: Then we are as cursed as our parents.

CLYTEMNESTRA: *(Looking back at* ELEKTRA*)*
As are all murderers in the house of Atreus.

(DEAD CLYTEMNESTRA *exits to the underworld.* ELEKTRA
follows ORESTES.*)

ELEKTRA: Wait for me Orestes.
(She exits.)

END OF ACT 6

ACT 7: ANTIGONE

(ANTIGONE *enters wearing a wedding-dress, carrying a toolbox and dragging planks of wood, random junk and plastic tarps.* DEAD POLYNEICES *enters from the other side carrying a bouquet of flowers. He has bloody bullet holes in his face. He stares at* ANTIGONE *then lies down lifeless.* ANTIGONE *begins to construct very crude large box, with the planks of wood, using a hammer, nails and rope.* NURSES *sing.)*

[The Complicated Love-Struggle Song]

(*The* NURSES *go back to work.)*

(CREON *enters wearing a tuxedo.)*

NURSES: Avoid excitement.

CREON: Yeah yeah.

ANTIGONE: Oh, hey Creon.

CREON: Hi Antigone.
Mind if I watch?

ANTIGONE: No, not at all.

CREON: You know, someone said this was happening.

ANTIGONE: Oh yeah?

CREON: Yeah.
And you know what?

ANTIGONE: No.

CREON: I didn't believe him.

ANTIGONE: Oh.

CREON: Yeah.
He said he was afraid of me,
Afraid of what I might do to him.
He said he ran a little while looking for me,
Then he ran back here.
Then ran a little while, closer this time to telling me.
Then ran back here.
Said it took him like twenty times to get to me.
Then he ran into me by chance.
Chance, can you believe it?

ANTIGONE: Yeah.
I saw him run away and come back.
Every now and then he'd ask me to stop working.

CREON: That's funny.
I wonder if he was more afraid of me or you.

ANTIGONE: I don't know.

CREON: It looks hard.
Is it hard?

ANTIGONE: It's not easy.

CREON: Do you even know what you're doing?

ANTIGONE: Not really, but I'll figure it out.

CREON: Like, what's that for?

ANTIGONE: What?

CREON: That big thing there?

ANTIGONE: I don't know yet.
I just grabbed whatever I saw I thought might be
    useful.

CREON: You thought that might be useful?

ANTIGONE: I thought so, yes.

CREON: No way.
I'll bet you twenty bucks you don't use that.

ANTIGONE: I'm not betting you Creon.

CREON: Okay okay.
Have you touched Polyneices yet?

ANTIGONE: No.

CREON: Good, you know when you do...

ANTIGONE: What?

CREON: You know.

ANTIGONE: Okay

CREON: Hey theoretical question: is it best to be right,
    feared or liked?

ANTIGONE: Right.

CREON: Without even thinking.
Snap, right, just like that.

ANTIGONE: What do you think?

CREON: I used to think liked.

ANTIGONE: What happened?

CREON: You.
Your father.
Your brothers.
My sister.
Death, war, sickness.
And now I'm the King,
Something I fought against my whole life.
And now I'm the King,
King Creon,
It sounds ridiculous.

ANTIGONE: A little.

CREON: Yeah, but here we are.

ANTIGONE: Yep, here we are.
Hand me that toolbox, would you.

CREON: This one?

ANTIGONE: What other toolbox is there?

CREON: I'm so stupid.

(CREON *hands* ANTIGONE *the toolbox.* ANTIGONE *looks through it.*)

ANTIGONE: Thanks.

CREON: Sure.
What you looking for?

ANTIGONE: Are you here to offer me carpentry advice?

CREON: I'm sorry.

ANTIGONE: So what do you think now?

CREON: About what?

ANTIGONE: Is it best to be right, feared or liked?

CREON: Feared.

ANTIGONE: Why?

CREON: I don't know.
It's the easiest,
You know

ANTIGONE: How about the most rewarding?

CREON: That too.
That too.
I guess.

(CREON*'s watch alarm beeps a little, he stops it.*)

CREON: Mind if I eat?
I got to take my pills with food.

ANTIGONE: No.

(CREON *takes out a bottle of pills and a boxed lunch.*)

CREON: You want some food?

ANTIGONE: What you got uncle?

CREON:
Some kind of sandwich I grabbed from the table.

Looks like just veggie.
How can anyone get full off this?

ANTIGONE: Sure, I'll take some.

CREON: And I have some soda here.

ANTIGONE: Any water?

CREON: Nope just the soda.

ANTIGONE: Okay.

(ANTIGONE *stops working and eats with* CREON. CREON *takes his pills with the soda.*)

CREON: The old blood-machine ain't what it used to be.
Avoid excitement, they say.

NURSES: Avoid excitement.

CREON: Yeah yeah.
How can a king avoid excitement?

(ANTIGONE *shrugs.*)

CREON: I got some cookies too.

ANTIGONE: No thanks.

CREON: For later though.

ANTIGONE: We'll see.

CREON: Alright, we'll see.
I know what that means.

ANTIGONE: It means we'll see.

CREON: You're getting kind of close to Polyneices there.

(ANTIGONE *moves.*)

ANTIGONE: This better?

CREON: Yes, thanks.

ANTIGONE: You're welcome.

NURSES: Avoid excitement.

CREON: Yeah yeah.
Cookies?

ANTIGONE: We'll see.

CREON: Alright.

ANTIGONE: So why did you fight against being King?

CREON: Well young lady,
My whole life I got the rewards of royalty
Without the burden.

ANTIGONE: So like laziness?

CREON: You could call it that.
But I think it's more than that.
Now, I have to make decisions for people you know,
for their welfare.
What gives me the right?

ANTIGONE: I don't know.

CREON: No, of course you don't,
Hence our situation.

ANTIGONE: Thanks for the sandwich.

CREON: And the soda.

ANTIGONE: And the soda.

CREON: Good girl.
Don't want to be ungrateful.

ANTIGONE: No I don't.
(She gets back to building.)

CREON: Back to work little worker ant?

ANTIGONE: Yeah, I have to do this by nightfall.

CREON: Antigone?

ANTIGONE: Yeah Uncle Creon.

CREON: Don't do this.

ANTIGONE: I have to.

CREON: Daughter, listen to me...

ANTIGONE: I'm not your daughter.

CREON: Yes, but you will be, when you marry Haemon.
You still plan on marrying my son right?
All dressed up...
He loves you, you know.

ANTIGONE: Why do all of us royalty marry each other?
All the people in the world, and we all marry each
    other.

CREON: Preserves the blood.

ANTIGONE: It pollutes the blood.

CREON: You will still marry him, right?
He does love you.

ANTIGONE: I love him, Creon.
And we'll see.

CREON: We'll see again.
We'll see.

ANTIGONE: We'll see.

CREON: He's waiting you know.
Everyone is there, waiting.
Everyone who's left in this city.
Everyone pestilence didn't cover with his murky
    excrement,
And drag into his infernal sewer.
Anyone holding on to life is there, waiting.

ANTIGONE: So they'll wait.
There's a D J, right?

CREON: Yes there is, not a cheap one either.

ANTIGONE: You can afford it.

CREON: I guess I can.
You're getting your dress all dirty.
That stuff is filthy.

Oh, and you shredded the crinoline for goodness me!
Arrrg. Think of the photos
Like some kind of zombie bride,
Arrg.

ANTIGONE: If Haemon wants to marry me,
He knows the woman he's marrying.

CREON: Yes he does.
This wedding is giving the people hope.

ANTIGONE: Hope, it's like a drug.

CREON: Drugs cure diseases.

ANTIGONE: That's medicine.
When it becomes an addiction,
We call it a drug.

CREON: Well, sort of.
Look girl, why don't you get up off the ground,
We'll just leave this stuff,
This junk.
You can get freshened up.
And we'll call this a temporary lapse in judgment

ANTIGONE: Oh, and you'll make a tomb for Polyneices?

CREON: No.

ANTIGONE: See.

CREON: He attacked our city, Antigone.

ANTIGONE: He had a right to the throne.

CREON: As did Eteokles.

ANTIGONE: Sure.
And if you didn't honor Eteokles with a proper burial
    this morning,
I would be doing the same for him.

CREON: Come out of there.

(CREON *tries to grab* ANTIGONE.)

ANTIGONE: Don't touch me.

ALL NURSES: Avoid excitement.

ANTIGONE: Look, I know your law.
I know what I am doing is a crime.
I know the punishment if I touch my brother.
It is not a mistake,
I am sorry if I am ruining your son's wedding.
But I don't know what else to do.

CREON: What about me?
What am I supposed to do?

ANTIGONE: Be feared,
Forget mercy.
Fill your hollowness with others' fear of you.
We all have to fill it with something.

CREON: What do you fill your emptiness with?

ANTIGONE: Envy, I guess.
Envy for people who don't care about life like this.

CREON: Come on.
People will surely be talking.

ANTIGONE: Good.

CREON:
Then you know it will be harder for me to be merciful.

ANTIGONE: I don't want mercy Creon
I wouldn't know what to do with your mercy.

CREON: You are not in control of your wits right now,
Wedding nerves we can say.

ANTIGONE: That's funny.

CREON: Look, even iron gives way to fire.
Wild horses become docile playthings.
Be like them horses Antigone.
You like horses, right?

ANTIGONE: Ismene likes horses.

CREON: Just drop the tools
And the wood,
Get cleaned up
And give a public apology.

ANTIGONE: Hey buddy?

CREON: Yeah.

ANTIGONE:
Would it be possible for you do more than kill me?

CREON: Yes.
I can.
I don't know what yet.
But I can.

ANTIGONE: Then start thinking of what it will be,
Because I am almost done with this thing.

CREON:
Everyone will see you as a criminal traitor to the state.
Not the adorable little girl saving truth from the
   chomping maw of nocturnal tyranny.

ANTIGONE: No sir, they will see you as a traitor.
But out of fear,
No one will tell you.

CREON: You aren't ashamed?

ANTIGONE: No.

CREON: You have become a hateful woman.

ANTIGONE: Well can you blame me?

CREON: I suppose not.

ANTIGONE: But I do nothing out of hate,
In spite of everything.
I only love.
I stay open for love.
And the world shits on me,
Then I open for love again.

CREON: You don't like horses?

ANTIGONE: It's Ismene

(*Enter* ISMENE *in a bridesmaid dress.*)

ISMENE: Hey.

ANTIGONE: Hey sister.

CREON: (*Cheek kissing* ISMENE)
Ismene, you look lovely.

ISMENE: Thanks.

(ISMENE *picks up the awkward thing discussed earlier and tries to nail it to the construction.*)

ANTIGONE: What are you doing?

ISMENE: I'm helping.

ANTIGONE: Don't be stupid, this is my job,
Your job is to find happiness.

ISMENE: Happiness without you, not likely?
(*She bangs her thumb with the hammer, this obviously causes great pain.*)

ANTIGONE: Put the hammer down.
And what is that?
What you nailed there?

ISMENE: I don't know.

ANTIGONE: Look at your hands, look at mine,
We are made for different work.

CREON: She's right Ismene

ANTIGONE: Help her up,
Brush her off.

(CREON *brushes dirt off of* ISMENE, *as* ANTIGONE *undoes the work done by* ISMENE.)

ISMENE: Will you have mercy on her?

CREON: If she goes much further I can't.

ISMENE: Then you will kill me too.

ANTIGONE: Ismene, there won't be justice if you take
the blows intended for me.
Go back to the wedding.

ISMENE: Mercy Creon, please, show her mercy.

ANTIGONE: I want no mercy.
I want Uncle Creon's full blow.

ISMENE: Stop rejecting me Antigone.

ANTIGONE: I'm not rejecting you sweetie.
I love you.
My death will bring peace,
Know this.

ISMENE: What kind of peace is there for me?

ANTIGONE: Ask Creon.

CREON: Go home girl.
You'll be fine.

ISMENE: I want to help.

ANTIGONE: I asked you to help, before,
And you said no.

ISMENE: I made the wrong choice

ANTIGONE: No Ismene, your life was always blessed by
delicate winds,
Charms from others.
And mine was always ghoulishly haunted by death.
The choices were made for us long ago.
Accept it, and find health, find an easy life.
I mean this, find things that can make you smile.

CREON: So what do you say Ismene?
Are you going to help Antigone consecrate Polyneices?

ISMENE: No.
Will she be killed?

CREON: If she doesn't stop.

ISMENE: What does Haemon say?

CREON: I haven't spoken to him.

ISMENE: And when you do?

CREON:
I am sure he will gladly plough less rocky fields.

ISMENE: That's gross.

CREON: Well…

ISMENE: Haemon loves her.

CREON: He loves the idea of her,
She wouldn't be a good wife.
Look at her, some kind of ogre bride, arrrr.

ANTIGONE: Go back Ismene.
It soon will be dark

ISMENE:
I will, but know that I leave my life here with you.

ANTIGONE: No you don't.
Get out of here.
I love you, Ismene.

ISMENE: I love you Antigone.

(ISMENE *kisses* ANTIGONE *then exits.*)

CREON: Smart girl.

ANTIGONE: Really?

CREON: Well, she obeys.

ANTIGONE: It's smart to obey stupid orders?

CREON: Yes. It's actually one of the smartest things
someone can do.

ANTIGONE: I'm not sure that's right.

CREON: It is, think about it, if…

ANTIGONE: Okay. Okay.
(She stands and stares at her unholy crude construction. She drops the last tool used.)

CREON: What's this?
You stopped?

ANTIGONE: Yes.

CREON: Well, thank you!
Finally some sense!

(CREON embraces ANTIGONE.)

ANTIGONE: I stop, only because I'm done.
I think it's ready.

CREON: Oh.

ANTIGONE: Yeah.

CREON: So we are there then.

ANTIGONE: Yes sir, we are there.

CREON: I was right about that piece,
You didn't need it.

ANTIGONE: Right again, sir.

CREON:
As soon as you touch him, you pass your verdict.

ANTIGONE: I know.

(ANTIGONE stares at CREON for a while.)

CREON: What's happening?

ANTIGONE: Just thinking?

CREON: About what?

ANTIGONE: I am dressed to get married.

CREON: Yes to my son

ANTIGONE: No, to death.
I ask not the stone for water,
For the stone cannot give what it does not have.

I ask not the snaky serpent to fly,
For without wings how can it?
Thus Creon lacks the compassion to understand.

CREON: Oh, no, I understand.
We are just on different ends of the understanding

ANTIGONE: Okay.

CREON: So what will it be?

ANTIGONE: See me, Creon.
See the last steps I take!
See the last rays of sun that shine upon my face.
See me come and take death as my groom.
And then see Antigone no more!

CREON: Okay.

(ANTIGONE *quickly grabs* POLYNEICES *and tries to put him in the construction.* CREON *kicks her face and she fall into the box.* CREON *then hits* ANTIGONE *with the toolbox.* CREON *in a panic, closes the construction and nails it shut.*)

(HAEMON *enters running.*)

HAEMON: Father! What are you doing?

CREON: Son, it's over.
(*He finishes nailing.*)

HAEMON: Is she dead?

CREON: She will be.

HAEMON: Then there is hope.

CREON: No son, no.
Let her go.
And don't hate me.

HAEMON: I don't hate you,
I am your son,
I accept all that comes with that hardship.

(HAEMON *tries to open the box.* CREON *pushes him away.*)

CREON: What are you doing?

HAEMON: Antigone!

ANTIGONE: *(In covered construction)*
I am here Haemon.

CREON: You can't save her

HAEMON: Why?

CREON: Because then your death will be next.

HAEMON: Really?
You'd kill me too?

CREON: Yes.
Well, I'd have you killed.
I know it stings,
But years will bring wisdom to this.

HAEMON: You make the laws and I obey?

CREON: Yes, right?
Is that wrong?
Is natural order fucked up?
Is it wrong that Fathers and Kings give structure to
sons and subjects?
Is that wrong?

HAEMON: No.

CREON: How could I let her live?

HAEMON: By not suffocating her would be a start.

CREON: And what would the people think?

HAEMON: Do people want tyranny or justice?

CREON: I don't know.
I don't.
Maybe they want tyranny that feels like justice.

HAEMON: That's ridiculous.
Pardon her,
Let her live Father.

CREON: Haemon, I gave her plenty of chances to stop.

HAEMON: You knew she wouldn't.

CREON: How am I to rule?
How can I provide for the welfare of the whole?
If the separate parts want special treatment?
I am trying to hold together a city,
A dying city, and she was tearing it apart.

HAEMON:
Only ignorance and hatred can tear apart a city.

CREON: You're so wrong son.

HAEMON: Is this your city, or is it for the people?

CREON: I decide for them.

HAEMON: I think you have it backwards.

CREON: She has to die.

HAEMON: Then she dies,
But when death visits,
He never takes only one.

CREON: Is that a threat, son?

HAEMON: No sir.

Good-bye Antigone, Happy Wedding Day.

ANTIGONE: *(Confined)*
Haemon, don't save me, this is right.

HAEMON: Yeah, I guess it is, wife.
(He exits.)

ANTIGONE: *(Confined)*
It is okay Haemon, I love you.
This will take my suffering envy away,
For all I know is suffering envy.
And I am nothing without it.
Take my body, my breath, my blood…

CREON: He is gone Antigone.

ANTIGONE: *(Confined)*
What?

CREON: Haemon is gone.

ANTIGONE: Oh...

(Enter THE BLIND SEER.*)*

THE BLIND SEER: Prince of Thebes, you know me.

CREON: Blind Seer, I know you.

THE BLIND SEER: So you're the King now?

CREON: Yes, how about that?

THE BLIND SEER: How about it.
I come here Creon, because once again,
You are on the brink of fate's fine blade.
But this time,
You are not an observer.

CREON: Excuse me.

THE BLIND SEER: This body has given you a sickness sir.

CREON: Polyneices?

THE BLIND SEER: Yes, it rots.
It pollutes,
It causes the sane to go mad.

CREON: What?

THE BLIND SEER: Can't you see, or are you as blind as I?

CREON: I can see.

THE BLIND SEER: Can you smell that rotten air?

CREON: No?

THE BLIND SEER: I guess we get used to our own odors.

CREON: Why have you come here?

THE BLIND SEER: Creon, honor Polyneices.
Pardon Antigone.

CREON: I can't.

THE BLIND SEER: Okay.

CREON: Have you come here to make me suffer?

THE BLIND SEER:
It seems the Kings of this place welcome disaster,
Not security.

CREON: What do you want?

THE BLIND SEER: What do you want?

CREON: I want peace,
I want stability.
I want everything to be organized and labeled.
I want all these sicknesses to end.
I want everything to be clean and sanitary.
I want timely trains,
And balanced books.
I want to know that people are what they say they are.

THE BLIND SEER: Then you want to be a fool,
Who believes in the unbelievable.

CREON: Tell me what to do.

THE BLIND SEER: Die, Creon.

CREON: I die?

THE BLIND SEER: Don't we all.
(Exits.)

(NURSES sing, underscoring dialogue.)

[Song Of Reckoning]

(CREON frantically tries to open the box.)

CREON: Help! Help me!

Anyone. Help!

(THE CARRIER enters.)

THE CARRIER: What is it sir?

CREON: Help me

(THE CARRIER *helps open the box. Enter* HAEMON *carrying the body of* ISMENE.)

HAEMON: Father.

CREON: Son help me...
Who is that?

HAEMON: Ismene.

CREON: She took her life?

HAEMON: No,
You did.
As you do mine.

(HAEMON *shoots himself in the head.* CREON *rushes to his body.*)

CREON: No, son, no.
Oh my life is extinguished.
My line stopped.
I have exchanged life for cruelty.
I kill joy.
I have always killed joy and hope
I leave the world with nothing,
Haemon, my son.

THE CARRIER: I bring grief upon grief, sir.

CREON: Can it be worse?

THE CARRIER: Yes, Antigone is dead.

(THE CARRIER *pulls the dead body of* ANTIGONE *from the construction.*)

CREON: She died so soon?

THE CARRIER: Yes sir, I guess sir.

CREON: All around...are dead.

THE CARRIER: When it rains...

CREON: I must pray.

THE CARRIER: No one wants your prayers.

CREON: Is there justice sir?

THE CARRIER: None sir.

CREON: Then know, it is foolish to act against the corrosive powers of man.

THE CARRIER: Yeah, no shit.

CREON: Sickness lays with in us all.
Cruelty,
Selfishness,
The ability to not sympathize,
Will be the death of us all.

THE CARRIER: I guess.

(CREON *on the edge of having a heart attack shoot himself in the heart. The* NURSES *stop singing. Silence. The stage is lousy with bodies.*)

NURSE: That was the smartest thing he ever did.

NEW NURSE: So, that's it?

NURSE: No, there'll be more.

(Blackout)

END OF PLAY